Fund Director's Guidebook

Second Edition

Task Force on
Fund Director's Guidebook
Federal Regulation
of Securities Committee

Printed in the United States of America.

Library of Congress Cataloging-in-Publication Data

Fund director's guidebook.—2nd ed.
p. cm.
Includes bibliographical references.
ISBN 1-59031-296-1 (pbk.)
1. Mutual funds—Law and legislation—United States. 2. Closed-end funds—Law and legislation—United States. 3. Directors of corporations—Legal status, laws, etc.—United States. I. American Bar Association. Section of Business Law.

KF1078.F86 2003
346.73′06642—dc22

2003022228

Cover design by Catherine Zaccarine.

07 06 05 04 03 5 4 3 2 1

Contents

Foreword

This is the Second Edition of the American Bar Association Section of Business Law's *Fund Director's Guidebook* (the "*Guidebook*"). It is intended to assist directors of investment companies registered under the Investment Company Act of 1940 (the "1940 Act") in fulfilling their responsibilities. The *Guidebook* should be useful to directors of both open-end investment companies (typically referred to as mutual funds) and closed-end funds. Inspired in part by the *Corporate Director's Guidebook,* originally published by the Section of Business Law in 1978, updated in 2001, with the *Fourth Edition* currently in development, this *Guidebook* summarizes or incorporates relevant information from the *Corporate Director's Guidebook* and supplements that information with specific guidance on matters arising under the 1940 Act and other applicable law.

Since the initial publication of the *Guidebook* in 1996, there have been a number of significant developments affecting the responsibilities of fund directors, particularly the enactment of the Sarbanes-Oxley Act of 2002 (the "S-O Act"). The S-O Act was enacted in response to a number of high-profile corporate scandals that eroded trust in corporate conduct and seriously impaired investor confidence. The S-O Act contains sweeping reforms in a number of areas that affect funds, including extensive new corporate disclosure and financial reporting requirements. It also mandates highly prescriptive federal corporate governance requirements that significantly increase the authority and responsibility of the audit committee and significantly heighten the role and responsibility of independent directors. The S-O Act also increases auditor oversight and independence and establishes standards of professional conduct for attorneys practicing before the Securities and Exchange Commission ("SEC") in the representation of issuers.

Some mandated S-O Act requirements (set forth in Section 301 thereof) relating to the independence and the required functions of the audit committee are to be implemented through the listing requirements of the national securities exchanges and associations ("SROs"). The New York Stock Exchange, the American Stock Exchange and the NASDAQ have submitted to the SEC proposed amendments to their listing requirements with regard to corporate accountability and audit committees. Listed issuers must comply with the new listing rules by the earlier of October 31, 2004, or their first annual shareholders' meeting after January 15, 2004. The listing requirements implementing Section 301 apply to closed-end funds with listed securities. Although not directly applicable to open-end funds, these listing requirements may serve as a "best practices" guide. Legislation has been introduced in the U.S. Congress to make the Section 301 provisions applicable to all registered investment companies. In the *Guidebook*, references made to the listing requirements refer to those imposed by Section 301 of the S-O Act.

Other developments since 1996 have also been incorporated in the Second Edition. These developments include:

- new requirements for funds in the area of corporate governance, including SEC requirements applicable to the retention of independent counsel for independent directors, that were adopted in 2001;
- the Investment Company Institute–sponsored "best practices report" (the "ICI best practices report"), developed by an advisory group of fund directors, identifying a variety of practices beyond those required by law for investment company boards and independent directors to consider adopting;
- litigation challenging the independence of directors serving on multiple boards in a complex;
- expanded oversight and monitoring responsibilities of directors, including those related to:
    - the effectiveness of internal controls and compliance systems;
    - valuation and pricing;
    - portfolio transactions, including best execution, soft dollars and trade allocations (particularly IPO allocations); and
    - personal trading by advisory personnel and codes of ethics.
- developments relating to the manner in which fund shares are distributed and the sales practices of selling broker-dealers and third-party financial intermediaries including those related to:

    - increasing use of revenue sharing and directed brokerage to finance distribution; and
    - well-publicized allegations as to market timing and late trades.
- increased use of multi-managers and sub-advisers and outsourcing to service providers;
- the impact of the Gramm-Leach-Bliley Act of 1999 upon bank-related funds;
- the privacy requirements imposed by Gramm-Leach-Bliley;
- the anti–money laundering requirements of the USA Patriot Act of 2001;
- new rules requiring funds to establish and disclose proxy voting procedures with respect to portfolio securities and to disclose information as to their proxy voting records; and
- the rapid growth of hedge funds and private investment companies.

In the interest of "user friendliness," the *Guidebook* avoids using footnotes; however, a bibliography has been included for those interested.

The *Guidebook* uses the terms "fund" and "investment company" interchangeably. These terms also encompass each portfolio in the case of a series fund. In addition, for convenience, the *Guidebook* uses the terms "director" and "board of directors" even though many funds are organized as business trusts and thus have "trustees" and a "board of trustees." The term "independent directors" means directors who are not "interested persons" as defined in Section 2(a)(19) of the 1940 Act, and the term "inside directors" means directors who are "interested persons." These concepts should be familiar to the fund director. Statements made about directors and their responsibilities under the 1940 Act apply equally to trustees. In addition, terms like "investment advisory contract" and "investment management agreement" refer to the contractual arrangements between the fund and its investment adviser or manager that govern the provision of investment advisory and management services. The *Guidebook* covers both open-end funds and closed-end funds. Closed-end funds differ from open-end funds in that they do not stand ready to redeem their shares daily at net asset value and generally do not engage in continuous public offerings of their shares. Shares of closed-end funds are traded in the market and may be listed on stock exchanges. The differences between open-end and closed-end funds are discussed in Section 13. For convenience, commonly used investment company terms are defined in the glossary.

Task Force on *Fund Director's Guidebook*
Federal Regulation of Securities Committee
(2002–2003)

Cochairs: Diane E. Ambler, Washington, DC
Thomas R. Smith, Jr., New York, NY

Julie Allecta, San Francisco, CA
Jay G. Baris, New York, NY
Stuart H. Coleman, New York, NY
Paul H. Dykstra, Chicago, IL
John W. Gerstmayr, Boston, MA
James J. Hanks, Jr., Baltimore, MD
Allan S. Mostoff, Washington, DC
Paul Schott Stevens, Washington, DC
Jean Gleason Stromberg, Washington, DC
David A. Sturms, Chicago, IL
Earl D. Weiner, New York, NY

SECTION **1**

Background and Structure of the *Guidebook*

The 1940 Act embodies a pervasive regulatory scheme that contemplates an important and active role for fund directors. Because of this, directors should have a basic understanding of relevant 1940 Act provisions and of the scope and nature of their duties and responsibilities. Moreover, although fund management and fund shareholders have common interests in many areas, there are potential conflicts of interest between the two. Under the 1940 Act regulatory framework, the directors (particularly the independent directors) are responsible for monitoring the conflicts and representing the interests of shareholders. Although fund directors will generally work closely and cooperatively with fund management, directors—particularly independent directors—must exercise independent judgment.

The role of the board of directors differs in certain respects from the role of director of an operating company because of the external management structure typical of most investment companies. A fund is usually organized by a "sponsor," such as an investment management company, securities firm or financial institution. Investment advisory, administrative, distribution and other operational services are provided to the fund through contractual arrangements with other entities, some or all of which are typically affiliates of the sponsor. In addition, the fund's officers are usually provided, employed and compensated by the investment adviser or administrator.

This *Guidebook* provides an overview of the functions, responsibilities and liabilities of fund directors, both under the federal securities laws (including the 1940 Act) and corporate law generally, as well as information about the structure and operations of the board and its relationship to the investment adviser, the distributor and others important to the fund, including the SEC. The *Guidebook* is intended to assist directors in discharging their responsibilities by providing them with enough information to enable them to understand their duties and to ask the right questions. It is not intended to provide all the answers. Perhaps even more than the typical corporate director, fund directors should seek and rely upon the advice of legal counsel.

This *Guidebook* offers suggestions as to how independent directors can best fulfill their responsibilities by reference to industry practice and legal requirements as well as the experiences and perspectives of the members of the Task Force that drafted the *Guidebook*. It must be emphasized, however, that there is no single way that independent directors can best fulfill their responsibilities, and there is often no one preferred approach to many of the matters discussed in the *Guidebook*. Furthermore, the positions taken in the *Guidebook* do not necessarily reflect the views of every Task Force member in all matters.

SECTION **2**

Introduction

A. The Legal Framework

Investment companies are registered with the SEC under the 1940 Act, which contains stringent and comprehensive provisions that require strict adherence to stated investment policies and limitations, prohibit certain types of investments, restrict transactions with affiliates and regulate investment advisory and distribution arrangements. Regulation extends to such matters as composition of the board and election of directors, capital structure, portfolio transactions, custodial arrangements, fidelity bonding, selection of accountants, valuation and pricing of shares and portfolio liquidity. The 1940 Act also contains extensive record-keeping requirements and contemplates that the SEC will regularly conduct inspections of investment advisers, funds and fund complexes. The SEC has broad enforcement authority and a wide range of enforcement remedies through which it may impose significant penalties upon fund directors, officers and fund service providers.

Fund activities are also subject to other federal laws, notably the Securities Act of 1933 (the "1933 Act"), and the Securities Exchange Act of 1934 (the "1934 Act") as modified by the S-O Act. The 1933 Act is a disclosure statute designed to ensure that investors are provided with full and fair disclosure of material information concerning securities offerings and issuers, including funds. Funds must register offerings of their securities with the SEC by filing a registration statement that includes the fund's prospectus and statement of additional information. The 1934 Act regulates the securities markets and broker-dealers and imposes ongoing reporting and proxy requirements on public companies, including funds. The offer and sale of fund shares may also be subject to notice filing requirements and anti-fraud prohibitions under state laws.

Despite heightened focus upon the responsibilities of independent directors, the role of directors is still to provide oversight and not management. Unless provided otherwise, fund management should be an active participant in the decision-making process even when the board or the audit committee has the statutory duty to make the final decision. In this regard, it is entirely appropriate for management to make recommendations based upon their knowledge and experience gained through the day-to-day management of the fund.

Investment companies are typically organized as corporations or business trusts under the laws of a particular state. Directors of investment companies are subject to traditional standards of director responsibility under state statutes and common law. Although funds are organized under the laws of a number of states, many funds organized in corporate form are organized under the laws of Maryland, and many funds organized as business trusts are organized as Massachusetts or Delaware business trusts. The responsibilities and duties of fund directors under state law are discussed in Section 14.

The regulatory scheme makes possible many and varied sources of liability for fund directors and officers and service providers, particularly the investment adviser and the distributor (or principal underwriter) of the fund's shares. Liabilities may arise from private litigation or SEC, state or other regulatory proceedings. Historically, management, including the inside directors, has usually been more likely than the independent directors to be the target of private litigation or regulatory proceedings. However, the independent directors are by no means immune from possible litigation, including litigation brought by the investment adviser. The increased responsibilities imposed by the S-O Act may require greater scrutiny of directors' indemnification and insurance (see Section 15).

B. Structure of the Typical Fund and Role of Independent Director

Most U.S. investment companies are externally managed, and typically all service arrangements necessary for the operation of the fund are provided by separate legal entities. The fund sponsor (or an affiliate thereof) normally becomes the investment adviser and the distributor. It is the statutory responsibility of the directors of the fund—particularly the independent directors—to regularly review and approve the arrangements with entities selected to provide portfolio management, distribution services and various other services required to operate the fund. Directors—particularly the independent directors—also have significant oversight and monitoring responsibilities under both state law and the federal securities laws.

Under the 1940 Act, the independent directors of a fund play a vital role. The Supreme Court of the United States summarized that role in *Burks v. Lasker*, 441 U.S. 471, 484–85 (1979) (citations omitted):

> Congress' purpose in structuring the 1940 Act as it did is clear. It was designed to place the unaffiliated directors in the role of "independent watchdogs," who would furnish an independent check upon the management of investment companies.
>
> In short, the structure and purpose of the 1940 Act indicate that Congress entrusted to the independent directors of investment companies, exercising the authority granted to them by state law, the primary responsibility for looking after the interests of the fund's shareholders.

C. The Role of the SEC

The SEC actively monitors each fund's operations for compliance with the 1940 Act, primarily through periodic on-site inspections of the books and records of the fund and of the adviser that are required to be maintained and through review of disclosure documents required to be filed with the SEC. Inspections for cause may also result from any number of events, such as direct receipt by the SEC of an investor complaint, questions presented through a Congressional inquiry, problems raised during SEC review of a filing or issues identified by the SEC staff from newspaper articles, investment company advertisements or fund websites.

During an inspection, SEC examiners typically review the minutes of meetings of the board of directors. Examiners consider such matters as whether the board has been properly constituted, whether changes in the board were made in accordance with the requirements of the 1940 Act and whether indications of any significant problems have been noted in the minutes. If the minutes adequately reflect the board's deliberations, they can be a factor in demonstrating that the board has carried out its fiduciary duties under the 1940 Act.

Because the SEC relies upon the independent directors to oversee the funds' activities and protect the interests of shareholders, the manner in which the independent directors perform their duties is of paramount importance to the SEC. When a troubling situation, such as improper portfolio investments or valuation problems, comes to the attention of the SEC staff, the staff is likely to question the extent of the independent directors' involvement and deliberations regarding the matter. The SEC may require specific oversight or action by the independent directors as a remedy short of enforcement or as a condition to settlement of an enforcement action or granting of an exemptive order or interpretive relief.

SECTION **3**

Composition of the Board—The Independent Director

A. Desirability of Independent Directors Generally

The 1940 Act contemplates independent oversight and monitoring of investment company operations based upon principles of corporate democracy. The typical investment company, however, has no employees, and the primary loyalty and pecuniary interests of the adviser and other service providers generally lie elsewhere. The interests of the investment company and its shareholders are of undivided concern only to the independent directors. Their status as other than "interested persons" is intended to permit them to act with genuine independence in addressing conflict-of-interest situations. The S-O Act also contains director independence requirements primarily in connection with the audit committee (see Section 4.B). The ICI best practices report identifies a variety of practices beyond those required by law for investment company boards and their independent members to consider.

When mistakes or violations of law do occur, the independent directors are expected to investigate the matter on behalf of the fund and resolve the problem with the adviser or other responsible service providers in an appropriate manner under the facts and circumstances of the situation. Appropriate remedial action may include prompt and full disclosure of the problem to shareholders or, on occasion, to the SEC and possibly reimbursement by a service provider to the investment company and/or its shareholders. Other remedial action, such as implementing improved internal controls and compliance procedures, may also be appropriate depending upon the circumstances.

B. 1940 Act Independence Requirements

The 1940 Act provides generally that at least 40 percent of the members of an investment company's board of directors be independent, meaning that they not be "interested persons" as defined in the 1940 Act. The SEC has promulgated a special set of governance standards which apply to funds that have adopted Rule 12b-1 plans, issue multiple classes of shares, or rely upon widely used SEC exemptive rules to engage in certain types of transactions with affiliates (the "SEC governance standards"). As a practical matter, the SEC governance standards apply to most funds because few funds can operate without having the ability to rely upon one or more of the exemptive rules. The rules adopted by the SEC in 2001 require that a majority of the directors be independent. Most fund complexes have adopted this practice even in the absence of any requirement. The ICI best practices report recommends that at least two-thirds of an investment company's board members be independent.

The term "interested person" is defined under Section 2(a)(19) of the 1940 Act to include (i) certain categories of persons with interests potentially in conflict with the investment company, (ii) persons with any beneficial or legal interest in securities issued by the investment adviser or principal underwriter or their control persons, (iii) a registered broker-dealer executing transactions involving the investment company or a related entity, (iv) persons loaning money or other property to the investment company or a related entity, and (v) legal counsel for the adviser or principal underwriter. The term also encompasses persons with close familial or substantial financial or certain professional relationships with management. A person who has been convicted of certain securities laws violations, enjoined from engaging in certain securities-related activities or prohibited by the SEC or by court order from serving as a director because of willful violations of the securities laws is ineligible to serve as a fund director. The ICI best practices report recommends that former officers or directors of an investment company's investment adviser, principal underwriter or related entities not serve as independent directors. In addition, SEC rules require broad disclosures about independent directors, including information that could potentially raise conflict-of-interest concerns. Consequently, it is important that the status and relationships of a potential director be considered carefully by counsel prior to his or her joining the board.

Generally, directors are elected by fund shareholders in accordance with state law and the SEC's proxy solicitation rules. Under the 1940 Act, vacancies on the board, however, may be filled by the remaining directors under certain circumstances. Vacancies on a board generally may be filled by the directors (without a shareholder vote) if, after the new director takes office, at least two-thirds of the board has been elected by shareholders. If the number of shareholder-elected board members decreases to less than half of the board, a fund must hold a shareholder meeting for the purpose of electing directors within sixty days. Special provisions generally require a shareholder vote to fill vacancies among the independent directors subject to Section 15(f) compliance (see Section 6.E). This likely will require a special shareholder meeting because many open-end funds are not required under applicable state law to hold annual meetings of shareholders. In Maryland, where many open-end funds are incorporated, a fund's charter or bylaws may eliminate the need for an annual meeting of shareholders in any year in which election of directors is not required under the 1940 Act. Funds organized as Massachusetts or Delaware business trusts, which are governed by their declarations of trust, also are generally not required to hold annual shareholder meetings.

C. Importance of Maintaining Independence

The consequences of failing to maintain the requisite number of independent directors can be severe. The 1940 Act requires that certain matters and contractual arrangements—including the advisory and distribution arrangements—be approved by a majority of independent directors. An investment advisory agreement approved by an improperly constituted board may not be valid, and, among other things, the adviser may be required to return fees received under the contract or provide its services at cost. Similarly, payments made by a fund to its distributor or underwriter under a distribution plan that has not been approved by a properly constituted board may also be recoverable. To the extent the requisite number of independent directors has not been maintained, other board actions may be subject to challenge as well.

Changes in outside affiliations should be reviewed to help ensure that an independent director does not inadvertently become an interested person of the fund or become otherwise disqualified. The ICI best practices report recommends that independent directors complete, on an annual basis, a questionnaire on business, financial and family relationships, if any, with the adviser, principal underwriter, other service providers and their affiliates.

D. Considerations with Regard to Service on More Than One Board in a Complex

It has long been industry practice for fund boards to include directors who serve on more than one board in a fund complex. For complexes with a large number of funds, this is a practical necessity. Although there are areas of common interest among the funds, the directors must exercise their specific board responsibilities on a fund-by-fund basis. Broadened exposure to the operations of a complex can be valuable to a board member and provide a better context for carrying out board functions, such as serving the independent directors' "watchdog" role. Service on multiple boards also facilitates administrative convenience.

The SEC has taken the position that service on multiple boards of the same fund complex does not make a director an "interested person" under the 1940 Act. Maryland and other state laws provide that a director who is not an "interested person" under the 1940 Act shall be presumed to be independent under state law. The ICI best practices report recommends that investment company boards of directors generally be organized either as a unitary board for all the funds in a complex or as cluster boards for groups of funds within a complex, rather than as separate boards for each individual fund. In recent years, there has been litigation challenging the independence of directors who serve on multiple boards of funds within the same fund complex. None of these challenges has been successful to date.

The directors and fund management should carefully consider the appropriateness of serving on more than one fund board in a complex, taking into account the increased responsibility and workload as well as potential conflicts that may arise.

SECTION **4**

Board Committees

Boards of investment companies often find it useful and, in the case of audit committees and nominating committees, mandatory to appoint committees of the board to which specified functions and responsibilities are delegated. Other special or *ad hoc* committees may be established for special purposes, such as investigating allegations of wrongdoing or pricing or valuation problems, or in connection with a governmental investigation or unusual conflict situations. These special situations are not addressed here. Nor are the difficult issues faced by special litigation committees appointed to determine the proper course of action to take when derivative litigation is brought against directors.

Where specific responsibilities are legally assigned to the full board or to the independent directors, the board may ask a committee to consider these matters preliminarily and to make recommendations to the full board (or to the independent directors). If action is required to be taken by the independent directors only, any committee to which the matter is assigned for preliminary consideration should consist solely of independent directors. The full board (or the independent directors), however, must act upon matters where there is a legal obligation to do so and will bear full responsibility for the action taken. In other instances, a director who is not a member of a committee may generally rely upon committee action if (i) the composition of the committee is appropriate for its purpose and the committee has been properly constituted, (ii) the full board makes reasonable efforts to keep abreast of the activities of the committee and is kept informed of committee activities, and (iii) the committee acts within the limits of its authority under applicable law and charter provisions.

A. Audit Committees

The S-O Act mandates requirements for the audit committee in terms of its composition and its role and authority. The S-O Act requirements do not, however, supplant or lessen the importance of the 1940 Act requirements as to director independence and the extensive role of independent directors in the regulatory scheme of the 1940 Act.

1. Composition of the Audit Committee

Although not applicable to open-end funds, the listing requirements provide that each member of the fund's audit committee be independent according to specified criteria that are different from that under the 1940 Act. To qualify as independent, directors may not (i) accept directly or indirectly any consulting, advisory or other compensatory fees from the investment company (except director's fees) or (ii) be an "interested person" of the investment company as defined in the 1940 Act (see Section 3.B). Disallowed payments to an audit committee member include payments to spouses or children and payments for services to law firms, accounting firms, investment banks or similar entities in which the audit committee member is a partner or occupies a similar position. The SROs may adopt further similar listing standards regarding audit committees so long as they are consistent with the foregoing. As noted in the Foreword, the Section 301 provisions of the S-O Act to be implemented through the listing requirements are directly applicable only to closed-end funds with listed securities but may serve as a "best practices" guide for open-end funds. Furthermore, legislation has been introduced in the U.S. Congress to make the Section 301 provisions applicable to all registered investment companies.

Although there are no required qualifications for service on the audit committee under the 1940 Act, the fund must identify in its annual report filed with the SEC at least one audit committee member that the board of directors has determined to be an "audit committee financial expert" ("ACFE") as defined by SEC rule. Alternatively, if the fund does not have an ACFE serving on its audit committee, it must so disclose and explain why. If the fund has more than one ACFE, it may, but it is not required to, disclose more than one name. To determine whether a person is an ACFE, the board of directors must find that the person possesses specified attributes and has acquired such attributes through a broad range of specified types of professional experience. The board decision as to whether someone is an ACFE for these purposes and the decision as to the number or numbers to be named in the annual report should be made in a considered manner with the help of legal counsel.

The primary benefit of having an ACFE serve on the audit committee, according to the SEC, is to provide a resource for the audit committee as a whole in carrying out its functions. The SEC further states that the ACFE is not expected to carry a higher degree of individual responsibility or obligation than other audit committee members. To codify this position, the SEC provides a safe harbor provision in the audit committee disclosure item (Item 3(d) of Form N-CSR), as follows:

- A person who is determined to be an ACFE will not be deemed an "expert" for any purpose, including without limitation for purposes of Section 11 of the 1933 Act, as a result of being designated or identified as an ACFE pursuant to the disclosure item; and
- The designation or identification of a person as an ACFE pursuant to the disclosure item does not impose on such person any duties, obligations or liabilities that are greater than the duties, obligations and liability imposed on such person as a member of the audit committee and board of directors in the absence of such designation or identification.

The SEC states that the designation or identification of a person as an ACFE does not affect the duties, obligations or liability of any other member of the audit committee or board of directors.

The foregoing safe harbor provision will provide protection with respect to SEC regulatory proceedings and private litigation under the federal securities laws but not necessarily litigation under state law.

2. Role and Authority of the Audit Committee

The basic purpose of an audit committee is to enhance the quality of a fund's financial accountability and financial reporting by providing a means for the fund's independent directors to be informed as to, and participate in the review of, the fund's internal and external audit functions. Another objective is to ensure the independence and accountability of the fund's outside auditors and provide an added level of independent evaluation of the fund's internal accounting controls. The audit committee also seeks to identify problems in the fund's accounting, auditing and financial reporting functions and increase the likelihood that any problems so identified will receive prompt attention. Finally, the audit committee reviews the extent and quality of the auditing efforts.

The S-O Act provides extensive requirements for audit committees in terms of their role and authority. The listing requirements provide that the audit committee is directly responsible for the appointment, compensation, retention and oversight of the auditors. The audit committee is authorized to evaluate and, if necessary, terminate the auditor. In addition, Section 32(a) of the 1940 Act provides that independent auditors of registered investment companies must be selected for each fiscal year by a majority vote of the independent directors (see Section 8.F). In connection with the annual approval of the audit engagement, the audit committee must receive information from the auditors to enable the committee to determine the independence of the auditor.

The auditor is required to submit an annual written report to the audit committee that must include (i) all critical accounting policies and practices used and disclose all alternative treatments of financial information within generally accepted accounting principles, (ii) the ramifications of the alternate treatments and (iii) the auditor's preferred course. The auditor must also report any accounting disagreements between the auditor and management. The audit committee is responsible for the resolution of disagreements.

The audit committee should meet periodically with the auditor without the participation of management to review the reports of the auditor. In this setting, the auditors typically are asked whether there are any matters regarding the fund, its financial reporting and record keeping and its operations that make the auditors uncomfortable; whether adequate accounting systems and controls are in place; whether management has adequate staffing; and whether there is any weakness in systems and controls that needs strengthening and, if so, the auditors' recommendations as to such strengthening.

Because of concern that the management consulting services offered by accounting firms have created a substantial conflict that has eroded the independence of auditors, the S-O Act specifies a number of non-audit services that the auditor cannot provide, such as financial information systems design and implementation, bookkeeping and other services related to the accounting records or financial statements. The auditor also may not provide a variety of other non-audit services, such as internal audit outsourcing, legal services and investment advisory services.

An auditor may engage in non-audit services (including certain types of tax services) that are not on the prohibited list for an audit client only if the activity is approved in advance by the audit committee. Preapproval by the audit committee is also required for permissible non-audit services provided to the fund's investment adviser, and any entity controlling, controlled by or under common control with the investment adviser that provides ongoing services to the fund, if the engagement relates directly to the operations and financial reporting of the fund. The audit committee is not required to preapprove audit or non-audit services provided to an unaffiliated sub-adviser that primarily provides portfolio management services to the fund. The audit committee may delegate the authority to preapprove non-audit services to one or more members of the audit committee. Audit committee approval of non-audit services must be disclosed in the periodic reports filed with the SEC.

The lead partner and reviewing audit partners on the audit team are subject to a five-year rotation requirement. There is a one-year cooling-off period for anyone on the audit team who seeks to be employed in a senior financial management capacity with respect to the fund.

It is unlawful for any officer or director, or person acting under their direction, to improperly influence the auditor for the purpose of rendering the financial statements materially misleading. The SEC rules provide that, in the case of funds, persons acting under the direction of officers and directors of the fund may include, among others, officers, directors and employees of the investment adviser, sponsor, distributor or other service providers. The SEC states that conduct it believes might constitute improper influence includes (i) threatening to cancel or canceling existing non-audit or audit engagements if the auditor objects to the fund's accounting and (ii) seeking to have a partner removed from the audit engagement because the partner objects to the fund's accounting. The independent directors must take care to avoid engaging in conduct with respect to the auditors that could be construed as improper influence. In their discussions with the auditors, the audit committee should make inquiries as to whether anyone has tried to improperly influence the auditors.

It is unlawful for a fund to retaliate against an employee or "agent" who has provided information about possible fraud or violations of federal law enforcement authorities and others (so-called whistleblower protection). The listing requirements provide that the audit committee must establish procedures for handling complaints and for confidential, anonymous submissions by employees regarding accounting/auditing matters.

The listing requirements provide that the audit committee is granted authority to engage independent counsel and other advisers as it determines necessary to perform duties and that the funds must provide appropriate funding, as determined by the audit committee, for the payment of compensation in connection therewith.

B. Nominating Committee

The independence of a fund's independent directors is enhanced by providing that persons nominated by the board for election as independent directors be nominated by a committee consisting of the fund's incumbent independent directors. The SEC governance standards require independent directors to select and nominate other independent directors.

Even with a nominating committee, the investment adviser may still play a role in the selection and recommendation of candidates for election to the fund's board. The adviser has a legitimate interest in ensuring that the independent directors are qualified and are not unduly associated with competitors. On the other hand, the adviser should not be permitted to participate in the process in a manner that limits the independent directors' discretion. The nominating committee should be properly structured, with a designated chair and with procedures designed to ensure that, as a matter of appearance as well as reality, the selection of nominees is made by the committee.

C. Pricing and Other Committees

Other standing committees are sometimes created by fund boards to focus on specific areas. Thus, a board may have, for example, a pricing, legal compliance, brokerage and proxy voting committees. In each case, the purpose is to designate an appropriate number of directors as a committee to devote time to the particular matter under review and make a recommendation to the board. For example, a pricing committee may be involved in the fair value pricing of portfolio securities or may review the methodology used by a fund in fair value pricing (see Section 8.A). It also might review the credit quality of unrated securities owned or proposed to be owned by a money market fund.

As a best practice, a committee might be charged with responsibility for developing and recommending to the board a set of corporate governance principles applicable to the fund and procedures for conducting performance evaluations of the board.

SECTION **5**

Board Operations

Boards of directors should conduct their proceedings in a way calculated to encourage, reinforce and demonstrate the board's role in providing independent oversight of the fund's affairs and the performance of its investment adviser. Board practice will, over time, significantly affect the extent to which a board of directors is likely to discharge its obligations in a manner that effectively protects and advances the interests of the fund's shareholders.

No single operational style fits all situations, and there is considerable diversity of practice among fund complexes. A board's operational style may be influenced by many factors, such as the number of funds in the complex, the amount of assets under management and the fund's distribution methods. Each fund or fund group should develop a style appropriate to its nature and circumstances. Fund directors may find it useful to compare the practices of other fund groups as well as evolving practices in the corporate world. The ICI best practices report identifies a number of practices followed by fund groups in their governance activities, which may or may not be suitable for every fund board depending upon individual circumstances.

Independent directors should consider having periodic separate meetings to review the appropriate corporate governance policies and standards relating to the manner in which the board conducts its operations. Topics to be considered may include the size of the board and its overall composition, the frequency of the meetings, the adequacy of the agendas, the quality of the information being received, the adequacy of access to the personnel of the adviser and others, the adequacy of access to qualified legal counsel sufficiently independent from the adviser and its affiliates and the adequacy of continuing education as to board members' duties and responsibilities, retirement policies and peer reviews.

A. Board Leadership

The special responsibilities of independent directors serving on fund boards are defined by the 1940 Act and SEC rules. The S-O Act mandates expanded audit committee responsibilities and imposes additional independence and governance standards as described as in Section 4.

Fund directors must be aware of various practical means of enhancing the independence and effectiveness of their efforts. The role of chairman is typically filled by a "management" director, often the chief executive officer of the investment adviser. Where this is the case, the independent directors may wish to designate one of their number to act as lead independent director, which was recommended by the ICI best practices report. This director can serve as the focal point for other governance and operational practices enhancing the role of the independent directors, including matters related to the requirements of the S-O Act. These practices could include, among other things: (i) providing for regularly scheduled periodic executive sessions of the independent directors to review performance of the investment adviser and other matters; (ii) providing independent directors with a greater voice in the establishment of the meeting agenda; (iii) serving as the principal independent director contact for counsel, auditors and other service providers working for the fund, and (iv) facilitating communications between the independent directors and other constituencies, such as the investment adviser, the auditors and other service providers. The audit committee should designate a chairperson who could be the same person chosen as the lead independent director. However, directors may decide to have different individuals fill these roles in order to spread responsibility and ensure manageable workloads.

B. Size of Board of Directors

There is substantial variation in the size of fund boards. Each fund or fund group should determine optimum board size with a view to ensuring sufficient independent directors to perform the required oversight functions and effective functioning in terms of discussion and decision-making. When directors serve on boards for multiple funds in a common complex, factors that might influence board size include the number of funds, the range and diversity of investment categories and the complexity of distribution arrangements. If there is concern as to whether the directors can handle the responsibility and workload with respect to the number of funds, the board sizes may be expanded or the complex may add an additional cluster in a separate board. In accommodating these needs, board size should not be expanded to such an extent as to interfere with effective functioning by making full and free discussion of issues at board meetings impractical. Larger boards may make increased use of board committees to allocate the workload.

C. Director's Time Commitment

The time commitment expected of directors is a subject that should be reviewed by the board and communicated to existing and prospective directors. Directors should take care not to overcommit themselves, and nominating committees should consider a board candidate's ability to devote the necessary time. Directors should expect to attend, in person, all regularly scheduled meetings. Disclosure is required in the fund's proxy statement of those directors who attend fewer than 75 percent of the aggregate board and committee meetings during the prior year. Independent directors are expected to devote sufficient time and attention to the affairs of the fund or fund complex to permit them to prepare for, attend and participate in meetings of the board and board committees and to keep themselves generally informed about the fund's affairs. The time required varies widely. Fund directors should expect to devote appropriate amounts of time, depending upon the number of meetings and the number and complexity of the funds involved. In times of crisis, directors will be required to devote additional time.

D. Meetings

It is generally regarded as a "best practice" for directors to be physically present at regular board meetings. Under the 1940 Act, the independent directors are required to meet in person to approve investment advisory and distribution arrangements and the selection of independent auditors. Telephonic meetings are generally permissible under applicable state law and may be useful and appropriate for special or emergency meetings.

The number of meetings a fund board finds necessary or useful varies with the circumstances. Some boards prefer more frequent and shorter meetings. Others prefer fewer but lengthier meetings. Industry practice ranges from quarterly meetings—generally thought to be the minimum number of meetings necessary for fund directors to discharge their responsibilities properly—to monthly meetings in the case of some larger complexes. Other complexes have quarterly two-day meetings. With the increasing emphasis upon the role of the independent directors and the audit committee, the trend is toward more frequent and longer meetings.

Time at board and committee meetings should be budgeted carefully. There are occasions when the independent directors may wish to—or should—meet alone. The ICI best practices report recommends that independent directors meet separately from management in connection with their consideration of the fund's advisory and underwriting contracts and otherwise as they deem appropriate. Many of the duties imposed by the S-O Act mandate separate meetings of the audit committee. The participation of legal counsel may be desirable to help the independent directors address the issues at hand. Whether a meeting is structured as a special committee meeting or as part of a regular board meeting, holding such a meeting is an appropriate exercise of independent directors' rights. In addition, the independent directors may wish to meet informally from time to time to discuss fund matters and generally compare views.

E. Control of the Agenda

Matters to be discussed and acted upon by the board typically are determined initially by the investment adviser, frequently in consultation with a lead independent director or independent counsel to the fund or the independent directors. In any event, independent directors should have an opportunity to place items on the agenda and to influence the priority and amount of time allocated to various matters. A balance should be sought between the investment adviser's presentations and discussion among directors and representatives of the adviser. Directors should be satisfied that there is an overall annual or more frequent agenda of matters that require recurring and focused attention by the board or a committee thereof, such as review of investment performance, required continuance of contract arrangements, required regulatory approvals, review of other services provided by the adviser and other service providers and meeting with the independent accountants of the fund.

F. Procedural Standards Set by the Courts for Fund Deliberations

Courts have examined the actions of the independent fund directors to determine whether the directors' actions should be upheld in situations involving a conflict of interest between the investment company and the adviser and its affiliates. If proper procedures have been followed, and there has been a valid decision-making process, the courts are more likely to allow the decision to stand.

Various factors that the courts have cited in assessing the quality of the deliberative process (and, therefore, the weight to be given to director determinations and approvals) include, in no particular order: (i) the relative number of independent directors; (ii) the backgrounds, experience and expertise of the directors; (iii) the methods utilized in selecting and nominating directors; (iv) the extent to which the directors understand the nature of their statutory duties and responsibilities and are free of domination or undue influence; (v) the extent and quality of the information supplied to the directors by the adviser and the manner in which such information is presented; (vi) the nature of directors' deliberations and whether those deliberations are substantive in nature; (vii) the responsiveness of the adviser to director initiatives seeking additional information or suggesting alternatives to management proposals; and (viii) whether the independent directors have their own independent counsel and have utilized counsel or other qualified experts in reviewing information or considering matters that require special expertise. This is not to say that every factor need be present or has been present in the favorable court decisions.

In fulfilling their duty to protect fund shareholders, independent directors must assure themselves that they have received sufficient information and independent advice to enable them to engage in the requisite deliberations and to support any findings that they are called upon to make. In this regard, both Section 15(c) of the 1940 Act, with respect to investment advisory approvals, and Rule 12b-1, with respect to distribution plan approvals, explicitly impose upon directors the duty to request and evaluate, and make it the duty of the investment adviser or distributor (as the case may be) to furnish, such information as may be necessary for the directors to fulfill their duties.

G. Quality of Information

The quality of information made available to directors significantly impacts their ability to perform their role effectively. To the extent feasible, information submitted to the directors should be relevant, concise, timely, well-organized, supported by any background or historical data necessary or useful to place the information in context and designed to inform directors of material aspects of a fund's operations, its performance and prospects and the nature, quality and cost of the various services provided to the fund by the investment adviser, its affiliates and other third parties.

Whenever possible, information should be provided in written form sufficiently in advance of the meeting to provide time for thoughtful reflection and meaningful participation by the directors. Many advisers and legal counsel provide directors with annual guidance manuals as to their duties and responsibilities or annual contract review books and regularly apprise directors of recent relevant legal or regulatory developments. The ICI best practices report recommends that new fund directors also receive appropriate orientation and that all fund directors keep abreast of industry and regulatory developments. In order to learn more about the quality of shareholder services, the ICI best practices report recommends that fund directors, where possible, invest in funds upon whose boards they serve.

Directors should review, and may also ask counsel to review, draft minutes of the board meetings before approving them.

H. Disagreement

If a director disagrees with any significant action to be taken by the board, the director may vote against the proposal and may request that the dissent be recorded in the minutes. Under state law, a director is generally presumed to agree unless his or her dissent is so noted. Except in unusual circumstances, a dissenting vote should not cause a director to consider resigning. If a director believes, however, that information being disclosed by the fund is inadequate, incomplete or incorrect or that the adviser is not dealing with the directors, the shareholders or the public in good faith, the director should seek corrective action and consult with legal counsel (who has no material relationship with the adviser) for purposes of determining an appropriate course of action.

Directors who have a personal interest in a matter being voted on should consider abstaining but, in all events, should disclose their interest.

I. Independent Counsel and Other Resources

Independent directors may decide to retain independent legal counsel and other experts, or in some instances to employ their own separate staff, at the fund's expense to assist them in properly performing their responsibilities under the 1940 Act. The S-O Act listing requirements provide that the audit committee has the authority to engage independent legal counsel and other advisers as it determines is necessary to carry out its duties, and that the issuer must provide appropriate funding for the audit committee as determined by that committee. The ICI best practices report recommends that independent directors have qualified investment company counsel independent of the investment adviser and the fund's other service providers. The listing requirements provide that the audit committee have express authority to consult with the fund's independent auditors or other experts, as appropriate, when faced with issues that they believe require special expertise.

Whether to retain independent counsel for the independent directors is dependent upon a number of factors. The SEC governance standards impose an independence standard for any counsel that may be engaged by the independent directors. The SEC requires that, if counsel is engaged to advise the independent directors, the independent directors must determine at least annually that such counsel must be "independent legal counsel" free of significant conflicts of interest that might affect their legal advice. Counsel with no material relationship with the investment adviser or its affiliates frequently acts both as fund counsel and counsel for the independent directors. In other cases, the relationship of fund counsel to management warrants having the directors consider retaining independent counsel. The size and complexity of a fund group may also warrant retaining independent counsel who can focus upon the needs of the independent directors. In lieu of regular independent counsel, the board might consider independent counsel on an *ad hoc* basis with respect to specific matters. The decision to retain independent counsel may be a question of economics as smaller fund groups may not have the asset base to afford regular separate representation. There is no "bright line" test, but generally it is important that the independent directors have ready access to counsel who views the board (and, where appropriate, the fund), rather than the adviser, as the client.

Independent counsel and other experts can contribute to the quality of the deliberative process and the validity and adequacy of the independent directors' decision-making process. The presence of independent counsel has been taken into account by courts in analyzing the degree of independence of the directors and in considering whether independent directors have carried out their responsibilities. Sometimes the SEC requires independent counsel as a condition to granting exemptive relief.

J. Board Compensation

Neither the 1940 Act nor state law sets forth specific requirements or limitations regarding the establishment of directors' compensation. The directors of a fund are responsible for setting their own compensation. State law generally recognizes that directors are entitled to "reasonable" compensation. The ICI best practices report recommends that independent directors establish the appropriate compensation for serving on fund boards. Directors have an inherent conflict of interest in setting their own compensation, which is not reduced if the recommendation is made by the investment adviser. Directors should recognize that they have the ultimate responsibility for determining their own compensation and seek appropriate data necessary to reach a fair conclusion, including data on comparable funds, together with analysis of any special factors that may relate to the fund or fund group. Directors' compensation may take a number of different forms, including annual retainers and attendance fees for board and committee meetings. Deferred compensation plans, retirement programs and similar benefits are sometimes provided. The compensation paid to each director by the fund and by the fund complex as a whole must be publicly disclosed.

K. Term of Service and Peer Reviews

Neither the 1940 Act nor state law sets forth specific requirements on retirement policies. The ICI best practices report recommends that fund boards adopt policies on retirement of directors, and many boards have adopted a mandatory retirement age policy, typically at ages ranging from seventy to seventy-five.

Some boards have also implemented peer review procedures to assure a periodic review of the performance of the board as a whole and of individual members of the board. The ICI best practices report recommends that fund directors evaluate periodically the board's effectiveness.

SECTION **6**

Board Responsibilities with Respect to Investment Advisory Arrangements

A. Statutory Responsibilities

The 1940 Act contains important provisions governing the relationship between the adviser and the fund's board of directors in negotiating an advisory contract. Congress viewed these provisions as particularly important given the significant nature of this relationship and the inherent conflicts of interest between advisers and funds.

Section 15 of the 1940 Act governs the terms of an advisory contract and the process of entering into, continuing, amending and terminating the contract. After the initial two-year term, the contract may be continued "annually" if it is approved either by the full board of directors of the fund or by the shareholders of the fund. Typically, the contract is renewed by the directors, not the shareholders (which is a costly and cumbersome alternative). In addition, any renewal of the advisory contract must separately be approved by the independent directors at an in-person meeting called for the purpose of voting on the contract.

In entering into or renewing an advisory contract, Section 15(c) provides that it is the duty of the directors to request and evaluate, and the duty of the adviser to furnish, such information as may reasonably be necessary to evaluate the terms of the contract. The advisory agreement for each fund must be considered separately rather than on a complex-wide basis. The annual review of the investment advisory arrangements is commonly called the "15(c) process."

To provide a remedy for excessive compensation, Section 36(b) of the 1940 Act imposes a fiduciary duty upon the adviser with respect to the receipt of compensation for services, or of payments of a material nature, paid by the fund to the adviser or its affiliates. Section 36(b) authorizes actions by shareholders and by the SEC against an adviser (not against fund directors) for breach of this duty.

In *Gartenberg v. Merrill Lynch Asset Management, Inc.*, 694 F.2d 923, 928–29 (2d Cir. 1982), *cert. denied*, 461 U.S. 906 (1983) (citations omitted), the court articulated the applicable standard for determining whether an adviser has received excessive compensation in breach of its fiduciary duty under Section 36(b) as follows:

> [T]he test is essentially whether the fee schedule represents a charge within the range of what would have been negotiated at arm's length in the light of all the surrounding circumstances. . . .
>
> To be guilty of a violation of § 36(b), therefore, the adviser-manager must charge a fee that is so disproportionately large that it bears no reasonable relationship to the services rendered and could not have been the product of arm's-length bargaining. To make this determination, all pertinent facts must be weighed.

The Senate Report accompanying the enactment of Section 36(b) in 1970 states that:

> Nothing in the bill is intended to . . . suggest that a "cost-plus" type of contract would be required. It is not intended to introduce general concepts of rate regulation as applied to public utilities.

B. Factors to Consider in Carrying Out Responsibilities

Section 36(b) directs courts to give approval of the advisory arrangements by the board of directors such consideration as it deems appropriate. The excessive-fee cases demonstrate that a valid Section 15(c) approval process is an important factor that increases the likelihood that the fee determination will be upheld. The excessive-fee cases suggest that all of the facts and circumstances surrounding the adviser's relationship with a fund are appropriate for independent director consideration. In determining whether there has been a valid approval process, courts often look to the expertise of the directors, the extent to which they are fully informed, the care and conscientiousness with which they perform their duties and whether they are represented by counsel independent of the investment adviser.

Other factors the directors may consider include (i) the nature, extent and quality of the services provided by the investment adviser; (ii) the investment performance of the fund; (iii) the costs of the services provided and the resulting profits realized by the adviser and its affiliates from its relationship with the fund, including the extent to which the adviser has realized economies of scale as a fund grows; (iv) other sources of revenue to the investment adviser and its affiliates from their relationship to the fund and intangible or "fall-out" benefits that accrue to the adviser and its affiliates; (v) the control of the operating expenses of the fund; (vi) the manner in which the portfolio transactions of the fund are conducted, including any use of soft dollars; (vii) a comparative analysis of expense ratios of, and advisory fees paid by, similar funds; and (viii) the entrepreneurial risk and financial exposure assumed in organizing and managing the fund. Data, including profitability, should be provided on a fund-by-fund basis. Counsel can help guide the independent directors through the approval process.

In considering various factors, the court in *Gartenberg* notes that evaluating comparable fees and expenses alone will not satisfy Section 36(b) because a fund cannot move easily from one adviser to another. The court observed that advisers seldom, if ever, compete with each other for advisory contracts with funds, which weakens the weight to be given to rates charged by advisers of similar funds. As a result, the court focused its attention on (i) the nature and quality of services, (ii) the adviser's cost in providing the service (i.e., profitability), and (iii) the extent to which the adviser realizes economies of scale as the fund grows larger.

Courts generally have not "second-guessed" a board's determination as to the fairness of a fee structure if the board has employed appropriate evaluatory procedures and has given due consideration to all appropriate factors, including the profitability of the adviser. Thus, the courts have effectively applied a "business judgment rule" in the 1940 Act context. Court opinions in the excessive-fee cases (which are cited in the Bibliography) provide informative and interesting reading for independent directors and illustrate in detail the nature of appropriate board deliberations and the scrutiny applied to those deliberations if litigation arises.

1. Nature and Quality of the Services

The courts generally have identified the nature and quality of the services rendered to a fund by the adviser as among the most significant factors that a board ought to consider. Although many different services are typically provided by an adviser under the advisory contract with a fund, the primary service generally is portfolio management, except in cases where sub-advisers are employed for that purpose. See Section 6.C.

2. Profitability

Profitability is one of the most difficult factors to analyze in reviewing an advisory contract. Courts have closely scrutinized costs and profitability data and methodologies. In so doing, the courts have acknowledged that there are many acceptable ways to allocate common costs, each of which could lead to a significantly different result. A difficult issue in determining profitability is arriving at an equitable allocation of the adviser's overall costs and expenses among the various funds and any other clients for whom it provides services. In general, a court should not invalidate a cost allocation methodology reviewed by independent directors if the methodology has a reasonable basis. Information about distribution costs is relevant, but it is important to identify and distinguish the marketing and promotional costs incurred by the adviser and its affiliates. If the adviser prepares the profitability information (as is usually the case), the information should be consistent with the information used by the adviser for internal management purposes. Retaining an independent expert to assist in preparing a profitability study may prove helpful, especially to the extent the expert establishes or reviews the allocation methodology.

3. Economies of Scale

With respect to economies of scale, the courts have concluded that the basic test is whether the directors can satisfy themselves that the information that is available provides a reasonable basis for judgment that the benefits of any economies of scale are equitably shared by the adviser with the fund (e.g., through appropriately fixed "break-points" or, alternatively, by means of a fee structure that in effect incorporates economies of scale by virtue of a relatively low starting point which subsumes economies of scale throughout). The importance of economies of scale was reiterated in the SEC staff's 2001 mutual fund fee study, which stated that, if a fund or fund family is experiencing economies of scale, "fund directors have an obligation to ensure that fund shareholders share in the benefits of the reduced costs by, for example, requiring that the adviser's fees be lowered, breakpoints be included in the adviser's fees, or that the adviser provide additional services under the advisory contract." If the fund or fund family is not experiencing economies of scale, the SEC staff suggests that directors "seek to determine from the adviser how the adviser might operate more efficiently in order to produce economies of scale as fund assets grow."

C. Sub-Advisory Contracts

With increasing frequency, advisers are delegating some or all of their functions to one or more sub-advisers. Under the 1940 Act, sub-advisory contracts are regulated in the same manner as advisory contracts. This means that they must meet the Section 15 requirements described above (including shareholder approval). A number of funds have been formed with a manager-of-managers structure. Under this structure, the primary adviser maintains overall responsibility for the management of the fund (as well as certain administrative responsibilities) but allocates management of some or all of the assets to one or more sub-advisers. The SEC has granted exemptive relief to funds to permit this flexible approach without the fund having to seek further shareholder approval.

D. Other Contracts with Affiliates

When a fund engages the adviser or its affiliates to perform services such as transfer agency, custodial, valuation or bookkeeping services, special consideration by the fund board is required. These other service arrangements are generally permissible. Based upon positions taken by the SEC staff, it is prudent for the independent directors to determine that (i) the service contract is in the best interests of the fund and its shareholders, (ii) the services are required for the operation of the fund, (iii) the services are of a nature and quality at least equal to the same or similar services provided by independent third parties and (iv) the fees for those services are fair and reasonable in light of the usual and customary fees charged by service providers for services of the same nature and quality. Payments to the adviser or its affiliates for other services may be subject to the fiduciary standards of Section 36(b).

E. Change of Control of the Investment Adviser or Distributor

In the event of a change of control of the adviser or distributor, the fund's investment advisory or distribution agreement is terminated by operation of law. In these events, the 1940 Act requires that the board of directors consider the approval of new investment advisory and distribution arrangements, considering the relevant factors discussed in this Section 6 for advisers and in Section 7 for distributors. Any new management arrangement must then be approved by shareholders. In considering the proposal of the existing adviser or distributor to continue under new agreements, emphasis should be placed upon any changes in the surviving entity's plans generally with respect to the fund, including the manner in which the portfolio management, administrative, distribution and other services will be provided and the extent to which new personnel, methods and systems will be used.

Many corporate transactions, including the sale of an adviser or a parent of the adviser, are deemed to be a change of control, which triggers this provision. Typically, the parties to the transaction seek to obtain shareholder approval of a new advisory agreement before the transaction actually takes place. Often, the nature of the transaction makes it difficult to secure shareholder approval of a new advisory agreement in advance of the transaction. In this circumstance, an adviser can continue to provide advisory services to a fund after a change of control under an interim contract for up to 150 days, subject to certain conditions and determinations by the directors.

A change of control of an investment adviser often implicates Section 15(f) of the 1940 Act. This section provides a safe harbor for an adviser that sells or assigns its fund advisory business for profit, provided the transaction satisfies two requirements: (i) for three years thereafter, at least 75 percent of the fund's board of directors must not be interested persons of either the adviser or the predecessor adviser, and (ii) no "unfair burden" may be imposed upon the fund as a result of the transaction. Most acquisitions of advisers are structured to comply with the terms of Section 15(f). The predecessor adviser and the successor adviser each represent and warrant that the transaction will not impose an unfair burden upon the funds. In addition, typically, the predecessor adviser or the successor adviser undertakes to pay all the fund's costs associated with approving the new advisory agreement.

SECTION 7

Board Responsibilities with Respect to Distribution Arrangements

A. Importance of an Effective Distribution System

Mutual funds continuously offer their shares and are obligated to redeem their shares for current net asset value within seven days after tender of the shares. A fund's ability to suspend the right of redemption is very limited. Closed-end funds, which are discussed in Section 13, typically sell their shares through underwritten offerings or through subscription offerings and are not legally obligated to redeem their shares upon tender to the fund.

The creation and maintenance of an effective distribution system for a mutual fund's shares is an essential goal of any mutual fund sponsor—to build an asset base adequate for portfolio management, to create economies of scale and to offset decreases in fund assets attributable to redemptions. Distribution activities are typically conducted through a general or limited-purpose broker-dealer (referred to as the "distributor") that is registered with the SEC and the NASD. The distributor serves as a fund's principal underwriter and primary marketing agent. In the case of "load" funds, which impose a sales charge, the distributor is typically an affiliate of the fund's sponsor. The distributor may sell shares through its own sales representatives and/or through unaffiliated dealers or financial service intermediaries who enter into selling agreements with the distributor. The sales charges (or loads) are used to finance some or all of the costs of distribution. "No-load" funds sell their shares at net asset value without any sales charge (although no-load fund supermarkets may charge their own transactional fees). No-load funds typically sell shares through direct marketing arrangements and may depend heavily upon media and direct mail advertisements, with the distribution costs paid by the adviser or sponsor of the fund.

As with investment advisory agreements, distribution agreements between a fund and its distributor must be re-evaluated and reapproved annually by a majority of the fund's directors, including a majority of the fund's independent directors. No shareholder approval is required for distribution agreements unless they involve a Rule 12b-1 plan (discussed below).

B. Development of Distribution Financing Techniques

In 1980, the SEC adopted Rule 12b-1, permitting funds, subject to specified conditions—largely procedural—to incur marketing and promotional expenses. The SEC takes the position that a fund is not permitted to use its own assets to pay for any marketing or promotional expenses unless it has adopted a Rule 12b-1 plan. Utilizing Rule 12b-1, the fund industry has developed a wide variety of methods for compensating broker-dealers that sell fund shares. These include deferred sales charge distribution financing techniques designed to enable the distributor to recoup distribution costs over time. There has been increased use of "back-end" sales charges in the form of contingent deferred sales loads (CDSLs), payable from the proceeds of redemptions effected within a specified period after purchase, and ongoing asset-based distribution fees. Both financing techniques use Rule 12b-1 fees to pay the distributor for the up-front costs of selling fund shares on a deferred load basis. Many funds, including no-load funds, money funds and front-end sales load funds, also have established Rule 12b-1 plans to pay relatively low service fees (sometimes referred to as "trail commissions") to compensate sales personnel and others for providing ongoing services to shareholders. Service fee rates typically do not exceed 0.25 percent of net assets.

In recent years, distribution alternatives have multiplied. For example, funds are now permitted to issue multiple classes of shares with each class subject to a different distribution arrangement but representing interests in the same portfolio of securities. An alternative to the single (or one-tier) fund with multi-classes is the master-feeder structure in which one or more funds (the "feeder funds") invest all of their assets in another fund (the "master fund"). All portfolio management services are performed, and related costs incurred, at the master-fund level, with distribution and shareholder servicing costs borne at the feeder-fund level. It is possible to combine the two structures by having feeder funds issue multiple classes.

Today, many funds offer investors alternative sales charge arrangements combining, through multi-class and/or master-feeder structures, front-end and deferred sales charge methods, and utilizing different combinations of service fees, distribution fees, CDSLs and conversion features from one class to a lower-fee rate class once a specified maximum payment level has been achieved.

Investors can also buy and redeem shares of many funds through "fund supermarket" programs sponsored by third-party broker-dealers or other institutions. In a fund supermarket, the supermarket sponsor offers administrative and distribution services to its customers who purchase shares of a fund participating in the supermarket program. The administrative services include providing through omnibus accounts the type of shareholder service typically provided to shareholders by a fund's transfer agent and other service providers. This results in savings to the fund in that the fees which otherwise would be paid to the service providers are reduced.

The fund and/or the adviser (or an affiliate) typically pays the supermarket sponsor an asset-based fee. Fees characterized as distribution-related must be made pursuant to a Rule 12b-1 plan, and fees for administrative services may be paid outside of a Rule 12b-1 plan. Some funds adopt so-called defensive Rule 12b-1 plans to cover both the distribution and administrative aspects of the program. The determination of the purpose of the fee payment is a question of fact to be made by the fund's board of directors, and this determination requires careful consideration and monitoring.

Over the past decade, selling broker-dealers have increasingly sought compensation from advisers for distributing fund shares in addition to the compensation they receive from sales loads and Rule 12b-1 fees. Payments made by a fund's investment adviser, from the fund's resources, to finance the distribution of its shares are referred to as "revenue sharing" payments. Revenue-sharing payments generally are not a fund expense. The primary legal issue raised by revenue-sharing payments is whether the payments are paid out of the legitimate profits from the adviser's contract with the fund or whether they constitute an indirect use of the fund's assets to finance the distribution of its shares and therefore must be made in accordance with the requirements of Rule 12b-1. The SEC states that the directors, particularly the independent directors, are primarily responsible for determining whether revenue-sharing payments constitute an indirect use of the fund's assets for distribution.

Many funds disclose in their prospectuses information about their investment advisers' revenue-sharing payments to broker-dealers. The SEC staff is considering making recommendations to the SEC as to whether additional disclosure as to revenue sharing should be required or current disclosure further refined. In addition to revenue sharing, the SEC and NASD are focusing on other incentives that broker-dealers and their sales agents may have to sell one fund over another resulting from differential compensation and other conflicts of interest. Among other things, they are considering requiring disclosure in this regard on the confirmation statement for mutual fund sales.

Another development is the increasing use by some funds of a portion of the brokerage commissions they pay on their portfolio transactions to compensate broker-dealers for distribution of fund shares. Some advisers direct executing broker-dealers to pay a portion of the brokerage commissions to broker-dealers who sell fund shares but perform no execution-related services in connection with the portfolio transactions. The SEC staff has stated that it believes these payments are intended to compensate such selling broker-dealers for selling fund shares and may be a use of fund assets for distribution of fund shares that should be reflected in a Rule 12b-1 distribution plan. The SEC staff states that it intends to recommend that the SEC take action to clarify the circumstances pursuant to which this use of brokerage commissions (to facilitate the distribution of fund shares) should be reflected in a Rule 12b-1 plan.

C. Board Responsibilities

1. Regulation of Distribution Arrangements

Section 22(d) of the 1940 Act prohibits a fund, its principal underwriter or a dealer in its securities from selling securities except at the offering price described in the fund's prospectus. Rule 22d-1 permits scheduled variations in sales charges discussed in the prospectus so long as it is applied uniformly in a specified class. For example, load funds often allow fund directors and other specified classes, such as employees of the adviser and retirement plans, to buy shares on a no-load or load-waived basis. As noted above, a Rule 12b-1 plan is the exclusive means by which a fund may directly bear the cost of selling, marketing or promotional expenses associated with the distribution of its shares. Advertising and sales literature are heavily regulated by both the SEC and the National Association of Securities Dealers Regulation, Inc. (the "NASD"). The NASD Rules of Fair Practice regulate all types of sales-related charges, imposing regulatory maximums on both front-end and ongoing asset-based charges.

2. General Responsibilities for Distribution

Little guidance is found in the 1940 Act or in SEC rules or interpretive materials concerning the factors that should be considered by a board of directors in approving distribution arrangements and fees. Directors should understand the proposed plan of distribution—to whom and by whom shares are expected to be sold—and the distribution costs to be incurred. The board should periodically monitor the performance of the distributor and receive regular reports on the sales and redemptions of fund shares and the costs of the selling function. The directors should monitor policies and procedures of the fund related to the distribution of fund shares, including any policies related to the extent to which shareholders can trade shares frequently (i.e., engage in market timing). (See also Section 7.C.5 with respect to monitoring of sales practices.)

3. Oversight of 12b-1 Plans

As noted above, a Rule 12b-1 plan is the exclusive means by which a fund may use its assets to bear the cost of selling, marketing or promotional expenses associated with the distribution of its shares. Before a fund's assets can be tapped for distribution purposes, a Rule 12b-1 plan (and agreements relating to the plan) must be approved by the fund's directors. The procedural requirements of Rule 12b-1 specify that the approval must be made by the board as a whole and separately by the independent directors. Before any Rule 12b-1 plan can be applied to an existing fund (or class), the plan must be approved by shareholders. Thereafter, each agreement must be approved on an annual basis by the board in the same manner as the initial approval and must be terminable (without penalty) at any time by vote of the fund's shareholders. The board must review payments made under the Rule 12b-1 plan on a quarterly basis.

In considering the establishment or renewal of a fund's Rule 12b-1 plan, the board of directors has an express duty to request and evaluate, and the distributor has an express duty to furnish, such information as may reasonably be necessary to make an informed determination that the plan is or likely will be effective. To approve a Rule 12b-1 plan, the board must decide that the plan is reasonably likely to benefit the fund and its shareholders. A fundamental factor to be considered in connection with all Rule 12b-1 plans is whether the distribution method under consideration provides for a reasonable financing alternative under the facts and circumstances of the particular fund and the type of investor to which the plan is directed.

Directors should approach the consideration of the distribution and service plan and related agreements with the same care as they approach the consideration of an investment advisory agreement. If a distributor is affiliated with the fund's adviser, Rule 12b-1 distribution payments to that distributor may be subject to the fiduciary standards of Section 36(b) of the 1940 Act.

4. Review of Multiple Class Arrangements

The use of multiple share classes is integral to many fund distribution plans permitting shareholders to purchase shares under different load arrangements and permitting funds to pay for access to different intermediary distribution channels. Prior to issuance by a fund of multiple classes, a majority of the directors, and a majority of the independent directors, must approve a written plan required by Rule 18f-3 under the 1940 Act setting forth the separate shareholder service and/or distribution arrangements for each class, the expense allocation for each class and any related conversion features or exchange privileges. The directors must find that the plan is in the best interests of each class and the fund as a whole. In making this finding, the board must focus, among other things, on the relationship among the classes and examine potential conflicts of interest among classes regarding allocation of fees, services and voting rights. The board must also consider the level of services provided to each class and the cost of those services to ensure that the services are appropriate and that the allocation of expenses is reasonable.

5. Monitoring of Sales Practices

A fund is responsible for its own prospectus, sales literature, advertisements and other reports generated by it. A fund generally does not have direct legal responsibility for the activities of its distributor, selling broker-dealers, or other financial intermediaries involved in the distribution of the fund shares. The fund is also not required to determine the suitability of the fund shares for the customers of selling broker-dealers. The activities of broker-dealers are regulated by the SEC and the NASD. The dealer agreements that distributors have with selling dealers typically provide that dealers must comply with the applicable rules and regulations regarding the sale of fund shares, including providing the appropriate breakpoints in share transactions.

Improper sales practices may result in litigation or enforcement proceedings which can adversely affect the distribution of the fund's shares, even if the fund and its management are not responsible for the violation or involved in the proceeding. The SEC has addressed the role of directors and their responsiblities with respect to problems in connection with late trading and market timing allegations, as well as in the calculation of front-end sales load breakpoints. In this regard, the SEC stated that directors as part of their general oversight responsibilities should oversee operational matters in which problems have been identified. In the case of the late trading and market timing allegations, the SEC has requested fund groups to promptly seek assurances from their selling broker-dealers and other intermediaries that they are following all relevant rules and regulations, as well as internal policies and procedures, regarding the handling of mutual fund orders on a timely basis. The directors should monitor these efforts.

To monitor sales practices, fund management may request that the distributor report to it from time to time as to whether sales practice problems have been identified and whether the compliance procedures adopted by the distributor to prevent sales practice problems are adequate. Another way to monitor sales practices is to request information about any adverse SEC or NASD findings and investor complaints. The directors should monitor fund management's efforts in this regard as part of their general oversight responsibilities. See Section 10.B. As discussed in this Section, distribution arrangements vary considerably from fund complex to fund complex. Directors should address specific issues concerning monitoring of sales practices, including market timing issues, within the context of the manner in which the shares are being distributed.

SECTION **8**

Other Specific Statutory and Regulatory Responsibilities

Directors have specific responsibilities under the 1940 Act with respect to approval of a number of other matters besides advisory and distribution arrangements, including valuation and pricing of shares, portfolio liquidity, custody arrangements, fidelity bonds and joint insurance policies, transactions involving affiliates, certain special types of investment practices and codes of ethics. Again, legal counsel normally provides the directors with guidance in meeting their specific responsibilities.

A. Valuation and Pricing of Shares

Because the price at which a mutual fund's shares are sold and redeemed on any given day is based upon the next determined net asset value ("NAV"), and because asset-based payments such as Rule 12b-1 fees and most advisory fees are accrued based upon NAV, it is critical that fund assets be valued on a fair and accurate basis at least once each business day. Errors in valuation can lead to costly adjustments and, to the extent that shareholders suffer any material loss, the party responsible for the error likely will be required to reimburse the fund and its shareholders.

The board should approve the valuation methodologies used in establishing the daily values of the fund's assets and monitor the accuracy with which the valuations are carried out. Portfolio securities must be valued at market price in the case of securities for which market quotations are readily available. When market prices are not readily available, such as when trading is suspended or when the fund holds restricted or other illiquid securities, the securities must be valued at "fair value," determined in good faith by or under the direction of the directors. There may be times when there are questions as to the reliability of market quotations, in which case it may be inappropriate to consider the closing prices as "readily available," and fair-value pricing should be used.

Typically, funds determine NAV at the closing time of the principal market in which the portfolio securities of the fund are traded (e.g., the close of the New York Stock Exchange for an equity fund). Funds holding securities traded on foreign exchanges may have special valuation issues resulting from the fact that the foreign markets may operate at times that do not coincide with the major U.S. markets, resulting in the closing prices of foreign portfolio securities many hours old at the time of the funds' NAV calculation. If a significant event affecting the value of the foreign securities has occurred in this interim period, the fund should consider using fair-value pricing. This can, among other things, prevent short-term investors in mutual funds from exploiting price discrepancies that have arisen. Funds should continuously monitor for events that may necessitate the use of fair-value pricing. The directors should monitor and consider the adequacy of the fund's policies and procedures for continuously monitoring and identifying significant subsequent events that may necessitate the use of fair-value pricing.

B. Portfolio Liquidity

The percentage of an open-end fund's net assets that can be held in illiquid securities is limited to 15 percent (10 percent in the case of money market funds). A security is considered illiquid if it cannot be disposed of in the ordinary course of business within seven days at approximately the value at which it appears on the fund's books. Determining the liquidity of a security is primarily an investment decision that is delegated to the investment adviser, but directors may establish guidelines and standards for determining liquidity. Determinations as to valuation and portfolio liquidity raise numerous issues for fund directors, especially in the case of restricted and other illiquid securities, Rule 144A securities (that is, privately issued securities that may be sold in secondary market transactions to qualified institutional buyers), foreign securities and derivative securities.

C. Custody Arrangements

The 1940 Act requires that the securities of a fund be maintained in the custody of a qualified custodian. The directors have a duty to oversee the fund's custody arrangements. In addition, directors have specific obligations for monitoring certain types of custody arrangements, including the use of self-custody or affiliated custody arrangements, and foreign custody arrangements. Of particular importance are Rules 17f-5 and 17f-7 (which permit a fund to maintain its foreign securities with a foreign custodian or a foreign depository). Rules 17f-5 and 17f-7 permit directors to delegate responsibility for the selection of foreign sub-custodians and the monitoring of both these sub-custodians and foreign securities depositories. These rules contain specific conditions and require consideration of a number of factors and specific findings by the board of directors.

D. Fidelity Bonds and Joint Insurance Policies

Rule 17g-1 under the 1940 Act requires each fund to maintain a bond against larceny or embezzlement and requires that the independent directors approve the form and amount of the bond. A fund can purchase fidelity bond coverage jointly with other funds and their investment adviser and distributor so long as the independent directors approve the allocation of the premium to each particular fund after consideration of certain specified factors.

Funds also often acquire either or both (i) errors and omissions insurance to cover losses from negligent acts of persons acting on behalf of a fund for which the fund might be held responsible and/or (ii) director and officer liability insurance to cover amounts recovered against a fund's directors and officers and amounts paid by the fund to indemnify its directors and officers. Such policies also cover the costs of defending any claims brought against the fund, its directors or officers. Such insurance may be purchased jointly with a fund adviser, underwriter or other affiliate if the fund's directors, including a majority of the independent directors, approve the arrangement annually based upon certain specified findings. Any such joint policy may not exclude coverage for litigation between the adviser and the independent directors. The policy should allow for advancement of expenses if an action is brought against the directors. The policy also should be several so that if one director is disqualified from coverage the remaining directors are still protected. In recent years, some funds have purchased supplemental liability insurance with policy limits reserved for the independent directors.

E. Securities Transactions with Affiliates

The 1940 Act contains a number of restrictions with respect to fund securities transactions involving affiliates. The four principal provisions are (i) Section 17(a), which prohibits a fund from conducting principal transactions with affiliated persons; (ii) Section 10(f), which prohibits a fund from acquiring a security during the existence of an underwriting or selling syndicate relating to that security in which an affiliated person is acting as a member; (iii) Section 17(e), which regulates brokerage or agency transactions by a fund with affiliated persons; and (iv) Section 17(d) and Rule 17d-1 thereunder, which prohibit an affiliated person acting as principal from engaging in certain transactions in which the fund is a joint or joint and several participant.

The SEC has adopted exemptive rules relating to these provisions that set forth specific responsibilities for the independent directors. Each of these exemptive rules is premised on the responsibility of the independent directors to adopt and monitor the implementation of certain prescribed procedures to mitigate the effects of the inherent conflicts of interest in portfolio transactions involving affiliates.

F. Selection of Independent Accountants

The 1940 Act requires a fund's independent accountant to be selected for each fiscal year at an in-person meeting by a majority of the fund's independent directors. The selection of independent accountants must be submitted for ratification or rejection by fund shareholders at the next annual meeting of shareholders (if the fund holds such a meeting). Rule 32a-4 under the 1940 Act exempts investment companies from this shareholder approval requirement if the fund has an audit committee composed entirely of independent directors and the audit committee has adopted a written charter. In selecting fund accountants, the directors should consider the qualifications, reputation and independence of the proposed accountants, the identity and skill of the engagement team assigned to the fund and the proposed scope of the audit and fees. See Section 4.B for information as to the duties imposed by the S-O Act on the audit committee with respect to the independent accountants.

G. Certain Special Types of Investment Practices

The EC expects directors to make certain inquiries and determinations with respect to funds engaging in (i) repurchase agreements, (ii) securities lending practices, (iii) reverse repurchase agreements, forward commitments and similar arrangements and (iv) transactions in options, futures contracts, options on future contracts, forward contracts and other derivative strategies. These inquiries should focus upon the strategies being pursued, the scope of their use, the risks involved, the creditworthiness of counterparts, any valuation issues and whether the practices are being conducted in a safe and sound manner. See Section 10(C) for further information as to the director's duties to monitor the use of derivative instruments.

H. Fund Names

Section 35(d) of the 1940 Act prohibits funds from using misleading names, and Rule 35d-1 thereunder requires a fund with a name suggesting that it focuses on a particular type of investment, industry or geographic locale to invest, under normal circumstances, at least 80 percent of its net assets (plus any borrowings for investment purposes) in that investment, industry or locale. The directors should keep this requirement in mind when reviewing the fund's investment portfolio.

I. Codes of Ethics

Section 17(j) of the 1940 Act and Rule 17j-1 require that investment companies, their investment advisers and principal underwriters adopt and enforce codes of ethics reasonably designed to prevent "access persons" from defrauding the investment company with respect to purchases or sales of securities. Access persons of a fund include its directors and officers and certain advisory and underwriter personnel. To the extent a fund's independent directors have no actual knowledge of the fund's trading in specific securities, those directors are generally exempt from most aspects of the fund's code of ethics. Codes of ethics generally require reporting of securities transactions by access persons, prohibit certain types of transactions and require preclearance of certain trades. Procedures reasonably designed to prevent violations should be reviewed on a regular basis to help ensure that they are adequate to enforce the standards of conduct that are contained in the codes of ethics. In addition, directors should be familiar with the applicable codes of ethics of their funds' sub-advisers and other service providers and monitor their effectiveness. Boards receive reports at least annually of any significant violations of the codes and of the sanctions, if any, that are imposed, as well as certifications that procedures are in place to prevent violations.

Funds, as well as their investment advisers and principal underwriters, must disclose whether they have adopted a code of ethics contemplated by the S-O Act that covers their principal executive officers and senior financial officers and, if not, an explanation of why they have not done so. The S-O Act code of ethics addresses a broader range of ethical conduct than the Rule 17j-1 code. Issues to be addressed include (i) the handling of conflicts of interest between personal and professional relationships; (ii) full, fair and accurate filings with the SEC; and (iii) compliance with applicable laws and regulations. Although it is not required, the S-O Act-mandated code of ethics can be integrated with the code required under Rule 17j-1.

Each director must strictly comply with the applicable provisions of the code of ethics of the fund. Directors should seek advice of counsel before accepting special investment opportunities from anyone associated with the fund or the investment adviser, such as purchases of securities in initial public offerings and private placements.

J. Anti–Money Laundering

The USA Patriot Act of 2001 requires that financial institutions, including investment companies, adopt anti–money laundering ("AML") programs designed to make it easier to prevent, detect and prosecute international money laundering and terrorist financing activities. As part of such required AML programs, funds must adopt procedures to verify the identities of their investors and keep records of such verification. Rules requiring funds to report suspicious activity also have been proposed, but not yet adopted. The rules likely will be similar to those requiring banks and broker-dealers to file suspicious activity reports. A fund's AML program must be approved by the fund's board of directors. The board should periodically assess the effectiveness of a fund's AML program and implementing procedures as well as receive reports from the designated AML compliance officer responsible for monitoring the program. A fund may delegate certain aspects of AML program implementation to service providers but remains responsible for general oversight and conduct of the AML program.

K. Privacy Procedures

Under Regulation S-P, the SEC requires mutual funds to follow procedures designed to prevent the funds from sharing personal information about their shareholders with unaffiliated third parties. The board should monitor the funds' compliance with these requirements.

SECTION **9**

Disclosure Requirements

A. Disclosure Materials

The principal disclosure materials of a fund are (i) the registration statement and prospectus used in connection with the sale of shares, (ii) annual and semi-annual reports filed with the SEC and periodic reports sent to shareholders, and (iii) proxy statements used in connection with shareholder meetings. There are also special disclosure requirements related to proxy voting with respect to portfolio securities.

1. Registration Statements and Prospectuses

Mutual funds engaged in a continuous offering must register, on a continuous basis, the sale of their securities with the SEC. Directors have a federal statutory responsibility for the accuracy of a fund's registration statements filed with the SEC in connection with the fund's offering of the securities to the public. A director, whether he or she signs the registration statement, is personally liable for any material inaccuracy or omission in the registration statement, including information incorporated by reference from other filed documents, unless a defense is available.

The director's primary defense to registration statement liability is "due diligence." To establish that defense, the director must show that, after reasonable investigation, the director had reasonable grounds to believe, and did believe, that the registration statement did not contain any materially false or misleading statements or any material omissions that made the registration statement misleading. Actions required by the director to satisfy the due diligence standard will vary with the circumstances. Directors are well advised to satisfy themselves that, in preparing the registration statement, the fund management follows procedures reasonably calculated to ensure its accuracy and completeness. Directors should personally review the document for accuracy, with particular attention to those statements and disclosures in the registration statement that are within their knowledge and competence.

As discussed in Section 9.B below, funds are required to maintain disclosure controls and procedures.

2. Reports to the SEC and Shareholders

Funds must also file annual and semi-annual reports with the SEC and provide annual and semi-annual reports to shareholders, which include specified financial and other information. Funds must also file their complete portfolio holdings schedule with the SEC on a quarterly basis. This schedule must be made publicly available. Funds may include a summary portfolio schedule in their semi-annual reports to shareholders rather than the complete schedule. As a general rule, directors are not personally liable for the accuracy of these reports. They should, however, be alert for any material inaccuracies or omissions in the fund procedures designed to prevent such problems.

3. Proxy Statements

Funds generally must comply with the federal securities laws relating to proxy statements. It is advisable for directors to review such statements to ensure that, based upon their knowledge, there are no material misstatements or omissions. Directors, even independent directors who were not directly involved in the preparation of a proxy statement, may be at risk if they fail to exercise appropriate care in connection with the disclosure statement. Proxy statements involving fund mergers are also prospectuses filed as part of a registration statement and carry corresponding liabilities.

4. Disclosure of Proxy Voting

A fund must disclose in its registration statement the policies and procedures it (or its investment adviser) uses to determine how to vote proxies relating to portfolio securities, including procedures used when a vote presents a conflict between the interests of fund shareholders and those of the fund's investment adviser, principal underwriter or affiliated persons. A fund must file its complete proxy voting record annually with the SEC and must make the proxy voting record available to shareholders upon request. The directors should review these proxy voting procedures, with the goal that the proxies are being voted in the best interests of fund shareholders. The directors also should monitor the proxy voting record, particularly those votes which present conflicts.

B. Certification of the Accuracy of Reports Filed with the SEC

The S-O Act requires that periodic reports filed with the SEC must be certified by the principal executive officer ("CEO") and principal financial officer ("CFO") of the fund. Among other things, these officers must certify that they have read the report in question and that all financial and other information disclosed is materially correct. The rules require the CEOs and CFOs to make specified certifications as to their evaluation of disclosure controls and procedures and their disclosures to the auditor and the audit committee about the internal controls. They must also certify that information has been included in the periodic shareholder reports as to their evaluation of internal controls and any changes in internal controls. The certification requirement is intended to improve the quality of the disclosure that a company provides about its financial condition in its periodic reports to investors and is designed to ensure that CEOs and CFOs are personally involved in the review of reports.

Funds are required to maintain disclosure controls and procedures designed to ensure that the information required in SEC filings and shareholder reports is properly processed and reported on a timely basis. Funds, under the supervision and with the participation of the CEO and CFO, are required to conduct an evaluation of their disclosure controls and procedures within the ninety-day period prior to the filing date of each report requiring certification. Although the directors have no specific responsibilities in connection with the disclosure certification requirements, these requirements are core provisions of the S-O Act, and, as part of their general oversight responsibilities, directors should be knowledgeable as to the procedures established by the fund and its investment adviser for compliance with the certification requirements.

SECTION **10**

General Oversight Responsibilities

A. General Responsibility

Investment company operations are subject to many requirements flowing from statutes, rules and regulations, court and regulatory decisions and rules of self-regulatory organizations. Funds also have investment policies and limitations, including fundamental policies and limitations that cannot be changed without a vote of shareholders. Policies and limitations are set forth in the fund's prospectus, its charter and bylaws, in resolutions adopted by the board or as conditions set forth in exemptive orders issued by the SEC. To qualify for the "pass-through" tax treatment afforded "regulated investment companies" under subsection M of the Internal Revenue Code, funds must also comply with a number of highly technical tax requirements.

Fund directors do not manage funds on a day-to-day basis. As a practical matter, the directors alone cannot ensure that funds comply with the foregoing. The board typically delegates these responsibilities to the investment adviser, the administrator, the custodian and other service providers who are responsible for the ongoing operations of the fund.

Although the independent directors are required to act as "watchdogs" for the shareholders, they are not expected to discover compliance failures on their own initiative. Instead, they may satisfy their responsibility by monitoring the adequacy of management's internal controls and compliance programs. These responsibilities are heightened in the case of matters in which conflicts of interest exist or problems have been identified. The task of monitoring compliance involving the adviser or other affiliated persons of the fund falls primarily on the independent directors with guidance from their independent legal counsel.

Quite apart from regulatory compliance, the directors should carefully monitor the overall business operations of investment companies. This process has been described as one of "kicking the tires, looking for warning flags." This is usually done through a series of written and oral reports provided by service providers periodically throughout the year, often in connection with regular and special board meetings. Reports may respond to guidelines adopted by the directors pursuant to SEC rules, or they may respond to board requirements imposed in satisfaction of the overall duties of directors. Directors should review these reports with a view toward monitoring the effectiveness of compliance procedures. Frequently, monitoring involves considering issues that reflect on the quality of the adviser's services or the quality of other service providers' compliance with applicable rules and regulations or prospectus requirements.

The following issues of compliance and monitoring deserve special attention.

B. Monitoring Compliance Programs

It is important that investment advisers, as well as others to whom responsibilities have been delegated, maintain effective internal control and compliance procedures. Knowledgeable compliance and operational personnel, with established lines of authority, should be responsible for implementing compliance procedures. These personnel, who should understand the importance of effective compliance programs and the consequences of failures, should be accountable to senior management. A very important component of any compliance program is the support of senior management and their ability to foster a firm-wide commitment to the observance of sound practices (the so-called tone at the top).

There is no single correct way for boards to monitor compliance programs. Directors should understand the elements of effective compliance programs, including training programs and written manuals, checklists and procedures for portfolio managers, traders and other key personnel. Directors typically seek to learn about the structure of compliance programs and may require management to report regularly about how it adheres to operational requirements. Directors should also inquire about the due diligence efforts management employs in its review of compliance by third-party service providers with applicable rules and regulations and fund policies and procedures. Boards may find it useful to have periodic meetings with the senior compliance personnel to discuss compliance procedures and any deficiencies. Directors should also discuss the adequacy of internal controls and compliance procedures with the fund's independent auditors and internal auditors, if any. Under the S-O Act's mandated certification process, the principal executive and financial officers must certify that they have disclosed to the auditors and the audit committee all significant deficiencies in internal controls and any fraud, whether material or not (see Section 9.B).

The SEC has proposed rules requiring investment companies and investment advisers to adopt and implement compliance policies and procedures reasonably designed to prevent violations by funds of the federal securities laws and violations by advisers of the Advisers Act. Under the proposal, if adopted, a chief compliance officer must be designated to administer the compliance program. The compliance procedures must be reviewed annually by the fund and the adviser. The chief compliance officer would be required to furnish the fund's board of directors annually with a written report on the operation of the fund's policies and procedures, including any material compliance matters requiring remedial action. The proposed rule would thus require board oversight of the fund's compliance program but would not require directors to become involved in the day-to-day administration of the program. This proposal codifies a best practice observed by many funds.

Boards should require advisers to inform them when the SEC schedules an investment company inspection and the results of any exit interview. They should also require management to give them copies of any deficiency letter. The directors can then review with management the response to the deficiency letter and consider with management any issues that appear to require the board's attention. Similar procedures may be appropriate for NASD inspections of the distributor's activities.

C. Investment Oversight

Although fund directors are not expected to play an active role in managing a fund's investments, they are responsible for overseeing generally the fund's investment performance and monitoring investment practices.

Performance is obviously one of the factors considered by the directors when they review the continuation of the advisory contract. Directors should also monitor fund performance during the year. Management should provide directors with regular performance reports with references to appropriate performance measurement indices and the performance of similar funds. The directors should also require focused performance presentation meetings on a regular basis. These meetings should include special written reports and oral presentations by portfolio managers with opportunity for discussion with the directors. In monitoring performance, the directors should consider the adequacy of the investment staffing and resources provided by the investment adviser in performing its duties. If a fund's performance deteriorates, the directors should consider what steps, if any, appear necessary to address the situation. Some fund groups address the directors' concerns in this regard by establishing "watch lists," which identify under-performing funds and describe specific corrective measures they are taking.

The investment adviser is responsible for managing the fund's portfolio in a manner that is consistent with the fund's investment objective, policies and restrictions. As part of their general oversight of investments, directors should be alert for any material deviations from these requirements. Directors should also use this process to build their understanding of the risks inherent in the fund's investment strategies.

As part of the investment oversight, directors should monitor the use of derivative instruments. The SEC has emphasized that certain steps are necessary to enable investment company directors to satisfy their fiduciary responsibilities in connection with derivative instruments. Particular areas of emphasis that the regulators have singled out have included (i) prospectus and statement of additional information disclosure of policies and limitations regarding the use of derivative instruments, (ii) valuation of derivative instruments (which often are priced at "fair value" because market quotations may not be readily available), (iii) the establishment of liquidity guidelines to ensure that funds will be able to readily redeem their securities, and (iv) the establishment of adequate risk management and internal controls.

Regular presentations by management concerning fund use of derivative instruments are desirable. These presentations may include such information as the extent of the fund's investment in derivative instruments, the specific purposes of strategies using derivative instruments, the success of those strategies, the resulting risk exposure, the effectiveness of internal controls designed to monitor risk, and the extent to which such activities have (and in the future may) affect performance. In their review of derivative securities activities, the directors normally may rely upon knowledgeable individuals or experts, including those on the adviser's staff or outside experts. Generally, directors should seek to reach a comfort level with respect to the adviser's ability to utilize derivative instruments effectively and to manage any attendant risk.

D. Brokerage Allocation Policies

Portfolio brokerage refers to the commissions paid by funds on portfolio transactions. Brokerage commissions are assets of the fund, and the fund's directors are ultimately responsible for determining policies governing brokerage practices.

Generally, advisers are required to obtain "best execution" in brokerage trades. In this regard, the advisers should periodically and systematically evaluate and measure the quality and cost of services obtained from the securities firms with whom it has brokerage arrangements, as well as the quality and costs of alternative market venues. The manner and the environment in which funds operate are constantly evolving, as are the regulations governing fund and investment management activities. Fund directors should stay abreast of new industry and regulatory developments affecting how business is conducted. Best execution does not necessarily mean obtaining the lowest commission. One senior SEC official has defined best execution to mean "execution of client trades at the best net price considering all relevant circumstances" or, alternatively, "placing trades in ways that are intended, considering appropriate circumstances, to maximize the value of investment decisions." Although advisers have the primary responsibility for implementing brokerage policies and procedures, directors should review those policies and procedures to ascertain whether they are designed to ensure that the funds receive best execution of portfolio trades. Directors should be especially mindful of potential conflicts when advisers allocate brokerage commissions to affiliates of the advisers.

The fund's statement of additional information describes brokerage allocation practices and what, if any, research or services the funds receive for directed brokerage. For example, the statement of additional information may refer to an adviser's policies on obtaining best price and execution as well as such issues as the adviser's receipt of research services from brokers, directing brokerage to dealers for the sale of fund shares or for the reduction of certain of the fund's costs.

There is no single way for directors to determine whether the funds are receiving best execution. Management should provide written reports that contain the names of brokers to whom they have allocated fund brokerage, the average commission rate paid, the total brokerage allocated to each firm during that period and portfolio turnover rates. This information will assist the directors in monitoring whether brokerage allocation comports with the applicable prospectus disclosure and satisfies any guidelines the directors may have adopted. As brokerage commissions are fund assets, independent directors should be aware that they may direct the advisers to recapture portfolio transaction expenses for the benefit of the funds. For example, they may suggest that advisers conduct portfolio transactions through affiliated entities or under other arrangements whereby the fund would recapture a portion of the commissions or spreads paid in the transactions. Directors should evaluate recapture of expenses considering the value of the services received by the advisers through soft dollars.

The directors should also monitor the adviser's practices with respect to portfolio transactions conducted on a principal basis as in the dealer market. Fixed-income securities, including money market securities, are generally traded on a principal basis.

Many advisers pay fund commissions to broker-dealers who provide research or other services either directly or indirectly through third parties. These commission payments are typically referred to as "soft dollars" because the advisers pay for the research and services with fund commissions rather than with cash. Section 28(e) of the 1934 Act establishes a "safe harbor" for soft dollars related to research. The law provides that advisers with investment discretion will not be deemed to have breached their fiduciary duty to their clients solely by having the account pay more than the lowest available commission if the adviser determines in good faith that the commission is reasonable in relation to the value of brokerage and research services provided.

The use of fund brokerage to pay direct fund expenses may require special disclosure in the fund's financial statements. The directors have a responsibility to monitor the use of fund brokerage to ensure that (i) the fund, and not the adviser, obtains the benefits derived from any use of its brokerage commissions not within the Section 28(e) safe harbor and (ii) the use of fund brokerage is consistent with the stated policies of the fund with respect to soft dollar transactions.

The SEC has provided regulatory guidance to funds and advisers, in the form of releases and enforcement actions, as to the standards of acceptable brokerage practices. The SEC staff pays particular attention to the conduct of portfolio transactions in its inspection program. In examinations of broker-dealers and advisers to learn about industry best execution practices, the SEC concluded that, although there were no major abuses involving mutual funds, some advisers did not keep adequate records documenting soft dollar activities; disclosure was lacking, and internal controls of some advisers were inadequate. The SEC has encouraged fund directors to be vigilant in monitoring brokerage and soft dollar practices, including monitoring conflicts of interest that may exist between a fund and its adviser resulting from soft dollar arrangements. The SEC staff has stated that it may be appropriate for Congress to reconsider Section 28(e) or, alternatively, to amend the provision to narrow the scope of this safe harbor.

See Section 7.B for information related to the use of brokerage commissions to compensate broker-dealers for distribution of fund shares.

E. Trade Allocation

Directors should monitor potential conflicts arising out of allocation of trades both among the adviser's various clients and as between the adviser's proprietary accounts and those of its clients. Conflicts of interest can arise particularly in situations involving initial public offerings (IPOs) or thinly traded stocks. Advisers may "bunch," or aggregate, trades of various accounts (including proprietary accounts) provided that they have established procedures designed to ensure fair allocation of trades among accounts if the trades cannot be fully executed. Directors should review the procedures that advisers use to avoid these conflicts to ensure that the funds are not being improperly penalized or that the advisers do not improperly benefit from their allocations.

Independent directors should generally not accept special investment opportunities from fund advisers. In an enforcement action brought against fund directors who accepted IPO allocations, the SEC alleged that the IPO allocations were improper because they gave the directors potentially profitable opportunities that rightfully belonged to the funds and that IPO allocations to independent directors could also compromise their independence.

F. Possible Need for Firewalls

In some cases, advisers may adopt procedures designed to create a firewall between the portfolio personnel who may have access to inside information and other personnel in the fund complex. Directors of funds whose activities could result in fund personnel receiving inside information—for example, when serving on a creditors' committee in a bankruptcy proceeding—should be mindful of the need for procedures to prevent the misuse of such information as part of their monitoring of investment practices.

G. Insider Trading

There may be times when investment advisers, in the course of managing fund assets, obtain material, nonpublic information. Insiders, including fund directors, are prohibited from purchasing or selling securities when they possess material, nonpublic information about the issuer and from "tipping" or disclosing such information to others who may use it in trading. Giving others recommendations to buy or sell while in possession of such information is also prohibited.

Although fund directors are privy to a wide array of information about their funds, they normally do not have access to the type of inside information usually available to directors of business corporations. Nonetheless, they may become privy to nonpublic information with respect to the fund itself or with respect to issuers of portfolio securities, such as information pertaining to a prospective tender offer or to a bankrupt issuer.

Purchasing or selling securities based upon this kind of confidential information, or merely passing the information on to someone else who acts on that information, is illegal. Insider trading by a director may result in criminal prosecution, disgorgement of profits, fines and other sanctions in actions instituted by the SEC. Similarly, directors should also exercise caution that information learned through their service as officers or directors of public companies is not improperly communicated to the fund and its affiliates.

See Section 13 for more information about prohibitions on insider trading relating to the fund's own securities.

H. Business Continuity Planning

Funds and their service providers should maintain comprehensive and viable business continuity plans in the event of large-scale disruptions in the fund's operations and those of its adviser and other service providers. The plans should be designed to achieve maximum business continuity in the event of a variety of contingencies, including long-term major disruptions. The plans must be reviewed and updated continuously. The directors should be informed periodically of the business continuity program and should consider its adequacy.

SECTION **11**

Role of the Board in Extraordinary or Emergency Situations

Mutual funds are susceptible to extraordinary or emergency situations as a result of their constant exposure to securities markets and their daily obligations with respect to the sale and redemption of their shares. The types of extraordinary or emergency situations are limited only by the imagination. A problem could affect the entire industry, a portion of the industry or just an individual fund or fund complex. An example of an industry-wide event would be a computer failure on a major trading facility. Severe weather disaster in a particular region of the country would affect just the funds in that region when, for example, mail cannot be delivered, complicating the proper pricing of purchase orders. On the other hand, the failure of a fund complex computer system would affect only the funds in that complex. A flood of redemption requests, generated by news or rumor, might exceed a fund's capacity to handle the situation. A money market fund may find itself in imminent danger of breaking the $1.00 net asset value. An employee, by means of false entries (for example, forged redemption requests) may have embezzled millions of dollars.

Response to an emergency situation will depend in large measure upon the nature of the problem. The independent directors should monitor whether fund management has contingency plans in place so that appropriate measures can be taken on an expedited basis in response to matters that may arise and so that all significant persons and entities involved in fund management and operations can be, and are, quickly informed. Depending upon the situation, a telephonic or in-person meeting of the directors with fund management and counsel may be appropriate. Situations that place the fund and its manager in an adversarial position increase the need for the independent directors to consult their own legal counsel.

In addition to notification of directors, fund counsel and fund personnel, certain situations (such as an inability to satisfy redemption requests) may also require immediate notification of the SEC staff and fund shareholders. Where a problem is industry-wide, or affects a sizeable fund population, the SEC will quickly become aware of the problem, and the resolution will most likely be uniform for all affected funds. In that situation, the primary responsibility of fund management is to keep current with developments and be ready to act in accordance with them. The relative importance of the matter will determine when or whether shareholders should be notified.

A. Statutory, Regulatory or Related Problems

The independent directors may be confronted with a situation involving a statutory, regulatory or other violation on the part of the fund. Examples include the making of prohibited investments, the engaging in prohibited affiliated transactions, the failure to observe board-approved guidelines, sales practice violations or a state blue sky registration violation. Because of the external management structure of the typical fund, resolution of the matter will probably require negotiation with the investment adviser, the distributor or some other service provider responsible for the matter. Under these circumstances, the independent directors should consider consulting with legal counsel that is independent of the service provider involved and such other experts as they deem appropriate. Resolution of the matter may involve negotiating some form of settlement or corrective action with the responsible entity and determining whether the relevant regulatory authorities and shareholders should be notified of the problem and the manner in which it was resolved.

Independent directors should clearly establish with fund management that the directors expect to be promptly notified of any statutory, regulatory or related problems or violations.

B. Standards of Professional Conduct for Attorneys

By rule, as mandated by the S-O Act, the SEC has established standards of professional conduct for attorneys who appear or practice before the SEC on behalf of issuers, including investment companies. The rule requires an attorney "appearing and practicing" before the SEC in the representation of an issuer to report evidence of a material violation of securities laws or fiduciary duties arising under federal or state laws, or similar violation by the issuer or any agent thereof (such as the investment adviser for a fund), that the attorney "reasonably believes" has occurred, is occurring or is about to occur. According to the SEC, an attorney employed by an investment adviser to an investment company who prepares or assists in the preparation of materials filed with the SEC on behalf of the fund is considered to be representing the investment company before the SEC.

Reports of a violation must be made to the chief legal counsel ("CLO") or to both the CLO and the CEO of the issuer (or their equivalents). After making a reasonably appropriate inquiry, a CLO must determine whether a material violation has occurred, is ongoing or is about to occur and must notify the reporting attorney of this determination. If the CLO determines that a material violation has occurred, is occurring or is about to occur, he or she must take reasonable steps to cause the issuer to adopt an appropriate response. If the reporting attorney believes that the CLO has not responded appropriately, the reporting attorney is required to report the evidence to the audit committee, another committee of independent directors or the full board of directors. Under a proposed rule of the SEC, in certain circumstances, the reporting attorney would be required to withdraw from representing the fund if he or she did not receive an appropriate response, and the fund would be required to report the withdrawal and related circumstances to the SEC.

Issuers are allowed to establish a qualified legal compliance committee ("QLCC") composed of at least one member of the audit committee (or, if the issuer has no audit committee, one member from an equivalent committee of independent directors) and two or more additional independent directors for the purpose of investigating attorney reports of material violations. The rules also permit the issuer's audit committee to serve as the QLCC. This provides an alternative system for reporting evidence of material violations. An attorney reporting evidence of a material violation to a QLCC has satisfied his or her reporting obligation and is not required to assess the issuer's response thereto. The QLCC decides whether an investigation is necessary and, if so, initiates an investigation. The QLCC has the authority and responsibility to recommend that the issuer implement an appropriate response to the evidence of a material violation. The QLCC also has the authority to notify the SEC in the event that the issuer fails in any material respect to implement an appropriate response.

The directors should be knowledgeable as to and monitor the procedures established by the fund and its investment adviser for confidentially receiving, investigating and retaining reports of a material violation. The directors must participate in the decision as to whether a QLCC should be established. The principal advantage of a QLCC is that it concentrates the decision-making with respect to attorney reports in one high-level group and avoids the problems that may be attendant to imposing the decision-making burden on the reporting attorney. On the other hand, membership on a QLCC imposes additional responsibilities on the independent directors.

SECTION **12**

Specific Board Responsibilities with Respect to Certain Special Types of Funds

A. Money Market Funds

Money market funds (sometimes referred to as money funds) are open-end investment companies that invest in short-term money market instruments and offer investors relative safety of principal, a high degree of liquidity, a wide range of shareholders services (including check-writing) and maintenance of a stable net asset value (usually $1.00 per share). Money funds are not protected by federal deposit insurance, and there is no guarantee that a money fund will be able to maintain a stable net asset value. Nevertheless, the ability of money funds to maintain a stable $1.00 share price has been important to their success.

Because of the importance of money funds as an investment medium for investor savings and reserve assets as well as the need to maintain a stable share price, money funds are subject to far more detailed 1940 Act regulation with respect to investment policies and portfolio composition than are other funds. Rule 2a-7 under the 1940 Act requires all funds that hold themselves out to investors as money funds to maintain their investments in U.S. dollar-denominated instruments and to meet detailed conditions regarding portfolio quality, maturity and diversification. These conditions are designed to limit a fund's exposure to credit, interest rate and currency risk. In addition, Rule 2a-7 permits money funds to use the amortized cost method of valuation and the penny-rounding method of share pricing to assist in maintaining a stable share price.

The role of a money fund's board of directors is of paramount importance in ensuring compliance with the requirements of Rule 2a-7. The following is a summary of the responsibilities of directors under Rule 2a-7, certain of which may be delegated to the investment adviser.

1. Board Findings

The board must determine in good faith that it is in the best interests of the fund and its shareholders to maintain a stable net asset value per share or stable price per share, by virtue of either the amortized cost method or the penny-rounding method, and that the money market fund will continue to use that method only so long as the board of directors believes that it fairly reflects the market-based net asset value per share.

2. Required Procedures

The board of a money market fund that uses the amortized cost method of valuation must establish (and periodically review) written procedures reasonably designed to stabilize the fund's net asset value per share at $1.00. These procedures must provide for (i) calculating the deviation of the fund's current net asset value per share from $1.00 at such intervals as the board deems reasonable in light of market conditions, (ii) periodic review by the board of the amount of the deviation and the methods used for its calculation, and (iii) prompt consideration by the board of what action, if any, should be initiated if the fund's amortized cost price falls below $.995 or rises above $1.005. Procedures must also be adopted with respect to using the penny-rounding method designed to assure that the money market fund's price per share, rounded to the nearest one percent, will not deviate from the single price established by the board of directors.

3. Oversight

The Board must exercise adequate oversight to assure that the adopted procedures are being followed. It should review periodically the fund's investments and the investment adviser's procedures in connection with investment decisions.

4. Portfolio Quality

The fund must limit its investments to those securities determined by its board to present minimal credit risk (which must include factors pertaining to credit quality in addition to securities ratings).

5. Security Downgrades

The board must act promptly if a portfolio security becomes ineligible for investment by the fund because of a decline in its credit quality. Directors must reassess whether the security presents minimal credit risk and must cause the fund to take such action as they determine to be in the fund's best interests. The board is relieved of this responsibility if the security is sold or matures within five business days of the adviser's becoming aware of the new rating and the board subsequently is advised of the adviser's actions.

6. Security Defaults and Other Events

If a portfolio security defaults, becomes ineligible for purchase or no longer presents minimal credit risk, the fund must dispose of the security promptly, unless the board determines that to do so would not be in the fund's best interest. This determination may take into account, among other factors, market conditions that could affect the orderly disposition of the security.

7. Delegation of Duties

The board may not delegate its duties related to the initial determination to use the amortized cost or penny-rounding method and the adoption of the required written procedures. The board may not delegate its duties in the event of deviation between the amortized cost method and net asset value using market quotations resulting in material dilution or unfair results or if such deviation is in excess of one-half of one percent. The board also may not delegate certain of its responsibilities in the event of a security default or downgrade except in those instances where the adviser determines that disposal of the portfolio security in question would not be in the best interests of the fund. Other duties generally may be delegated to the fund's investment adviser, provided that the board establishes guidelines, reviews them periodically and otherwise exercises adequate oversight.

The duties of money fund directors with respect to liquidity requirements (see Section 8.B) and investments in derivative securities (see Section 10.C) are heightened because of the special nature of money funds.

B. Funds Investing in Foreign Securities

With the increasing internationalization of the capital markets, there has been a dramatic increase in U.S. investor interest in non-U.S. securities and, similarly, a sharp increase in the number of U.S. funds investing abroad. Funds investing abroad include funds investing in the securities of a single country (country funds), funds investing in specific regions (such as Europe or Latin America), funds investing abroad on a worldwide basis (international funds) and funds investing both in the U.S. and abroad (global funds). A number of these funds have non-U.S. investment advisers or sub-advisers.

Investment in foreign securities presents several areas for special oversight, particularly custody of assets, portfolio valuation and liquidity and the timeliness of recognition of income and capital changes. To the extent the foreign securities markets in which the fund trades are not as developed or are less efficient than U.S. markets, or to the extent the volume of trading is lower than in the U.S. markets, questions are more likely to arise as to the appropriateness of the valuation of one or more portfolio securities or pricing issues resulting from the fact that foreign markets may operate at times that do not coincide with the U.S. markets (see Section 8.A). These factors also raise questions as to compliance with portfolio liquidity requirements for open-end funds. In fact, many funds emphasizing investments in foreign securities, particularly country funds, are organized as closed-end funds due to portfolio liquidity concerns. Another difficulty in administering funds investing in foreign markets is obtaining timely information as to matters affecting portfolio securities, such as the declaration of dividends and distributions. Directors have specific responsibilities as to the selection of foreign custodians of fund assets (see Section 8.C).

C. Funds Used as Funding Vehicles for Insurance Products

Variable annuity contracts and variable life insurance policies invest in mutual funds that, because of federal income tax limitations, do not offer their shares to the general public but are dedicated to insurance products or tax-qualified retirement plans and are required to satisfy special federal tax diversification requirements. The legal owners of these dedicated fund shares are the insurance company separate accounts, which are, together with the interests in the insurance products they issue to contract owners, themselves separately regulated under the federal securities laws. The 1940 Act places responsibility on the insurance company, and not the dedicated fund or its board of directors, to determine the reasonableness of aggregate insurance product fees and charges.

There are areas in which dedicated fund boards have duties directly to contract holders as beneficial owners of the fund shares. SEC rules and administrative positions require that voting rights attributable to dedicated fund shares held by the separate account be "passed-through" to contract holders and that fund shares held by the insurance company or otherwise not voted be "echo voted" in proportion to the contract holder votes received. Funds that sell their shares to both variable annuity separate accounts and variable life separate accounts (known as mixed funding) or sell fund shares to unaffiliated insurance companies (known as shared funding) must have a majority of independent directors, and the directors must establish and follow procedures to monitor for "irreconcilable material conflicts" that might arise among the interests of contract owners and determine any appropriate action to be taken in the event of a conflict.

The laws governing the approval of a mutual fund's investment advisory agreement do not specifically refer to dedicated funds or variable insurance products. However, where a dedicated fund is advised by an insurance company (or an affiliate of an insurance company) issuing insurance products investing in the fund, the interrelationship between the fund and the insurance company should be considered by the board of directors of the dedicated fund in this context. Also, the SEC staff has taken the position that a board of directors presented with approval of a Rule 12b-1 plan for a dedicated fund must look to the best interests of the ultimate contract owners, not the insurance company separate account nominal shareholders, and assure itself that the 12b-1 plan proceeds are being used for legitimate services supporting the indirect marketing of the dedicated fund shares through the insurance company separate account to contract owners.

The SEC and its staff have required insurance company issuers of variable insurance products to deliver to contract owners materials prepared by dedicated funds for their shareholders, including prospectuses, annual and semi-annual reports, proxy materials and other shareholder materials. Also, a court has suggested that owners of insurance products may have an implied cause of action against dedicated funds underlying their insurance products for breach of fiduciary duty.

D. Fund of Funds

Certain investment companies are organized to invest either primarily or exclusively in other investment companies. These "funds of funds" may invest in registered or unregistered funds. In light of fee layering and other abuses revealed by the funds-of-funds scandals of the early 1970s, Congress amended the 1940 Act to provide that registered fund investments in other funds are limited to 10 percent of the "top tier" fund's assets, except that open-end funds of funds can invest without limitation in other funds if the top-tier fund's portfolio is comprised solely of securities issued by other funds in the same complex, U.S. Government securities and short-term paper.

The directors of the top-tier fund in a fund-of-funds structure are generally not responsible for overseeing the operations of the funds in which the top-tier fund invests. As is the case with any investment company, however, directors should exercise a reasonable degree of care and diligence with respect to the top-tier fund's portfolio management and management's choice of portfolio securities. Moreover, in the case of a fund of affiliated funds, the directors of the top-tier fund must be mindful of the fees paid to the adviser and its affiliates from both the top-tier and bottom-tier funds and be satisfied that those fees in the aggregate are reasonable in light of the services provided.

E. Hedge Funds and Private Investment Companies

In recent years, there has been a great expansion in pooled investment entities that are exempt from the registration and reporting requirements of the 1940 Act. These exempt entities are largely private investment companies or so-called hedge funds. Although exempt from the registration provisions of the 1940 Act, private investment companies are subject to the anti-fraud provisions of the Federal securities laws, and, in recent years, such companies have been the subject of considerable SEC enforcement focus. The SEC staff has conducted an extensive hedge fund study and has made recommendations for the SEC to consider, which, among other things, would require hedge fund advisers to register as investment advisers under the Advisers Act and would require greater disclosure as to the operations of hedge funds.

Many mutual fund sponsors also sponsor private investment companies. The SEC inspection staff has stated that, because the adviser typically receives a percentage of capital gains for managing private investment companies, it may have an incentive to favor private investment companies over registered funds that have a lower advisory fee. The staff has stated that it will examine trade allocations as part of its inspection program to determine if the allocations are conducted in a fair manner. The staff has also stated that it is concerned about the possibility of manipulation resulting from the use of short sales by hedge funds when public funds have long positions in the same security. Advisers should have compliance procedures in place to address these conflicts of interest and potential for abuse.

F. Bank-Related Funds

In recent years, banks have greatly increased their investment company activities both with respect to their own "proprietary funds," which they manage, and "nonproprietary funds," which are managed by others and the shares of which are sold through bank retail channels and bank trust departments.

The Gramm-Leach-Bliley Act of 1999 eliminated most of the barriers between the banking industry and the securities industry that historically limited the extent to which banks could engage in the fund business. Today, bank affiliates that register as "financial holding companies" can engage in most kinds of mutual fund activity. For the most part, the SEC is the "functional regulator" of bank mutual fund activities.

Although the former restrictions no longer apply, directors of bank-related funds should monitor the relationship between banks and their affiliates, on one hand, and the funds that they advise or distribute on the other hand. Banking regulations or restrictions still apply to relationships between the banks and their affiliated funds and may present some compliance issues. Directors should inquire about potential conflicts and how management monitors them.

Sales practices are a particular concern for fund shares sold on bank premises. A number of the regulatory authorities and industry associations have issued sales practice guidelines designed to ensure the separation of fund sales activities from insured deposit-taking activities in order to avoid confusion between insured and noninsured products and to foster appropriate qualification, training and compliance programs.

G. Exchange-Traded Funds

Exchange-traded funds (or "ETFs") are hybrid investment companies that are registered as open-end investment companies or unit investment trusts but possess some of the characteristics of closed-end funds (see Section 13). Unlike traditional open-end funds and UITs, ETFs do not sell and redeem their individual shares as net asset value. ETFs list their shares on national securities exchanges, which permits investors to buy and sell individual ETF shares throughout the day at market prices which may be higher or lower than their net asset value.

ETFs offer investors the diversification and relatively low expenses associated with index investing, as well as the ability for intraday trading and short selling and certain tax efficiencies. In addition, unlike closed-end funds, shares of ETFs typically trade at or close to their net asset value. Currently, ETFs are limited to those that seek to track the performance of a specific domestic or foreign stock index. The SEC has not permitted actively managed ETFs but is considering industry proposals for actively managed ETFs.

SECTION **13**

Specific Board Responsibilities with Respect to Closed-End Funds

A. Overview

Registration of closed-end funds under the 1940 Act and their directors' duties under state law are substantially similar to those of open-end funds. There are differences, however, which largely reflect a few principal factors.

1. Differences Between Closed-End and Open-End Funds

Closed-end funds, unlike open-end funds, do not stand ready to redeem their shares daily at net asset value, nor do they normally engage in continuous public offerings of their shares. Closed-end funds do not need to maintain the liquidity of investments or the cash reserves needed by open-end funds to meet redemption demands, nor to engage in continuous offerings of their shares to offset redemptions. Like other corporations, closed-end funds may wish to raise capital through public or private borrowings, issuance of preferred stock and offerings of common shares. Requirements under the 1940 Act peculiarly applicable to closed-end funds recognize these differences by providing greater flexibility for leverage than is available to open-end funds and by permitting rights offerings for common shares of closed-end funds when they are trading at a discount to their net asset value.

Because closed-end funds do not need to stand ready to redeem their portfolios on a daily basis, closed-end funds generally are not limited by the SEC, as are open-end funds, in the percentage of their portfolios that may be invested in illiquid securities.

2. Regulation of Closed-End Funds

Liquidity to shareholders of closed-end funds generally is provided through listing and open-market trading on stock exchanges and NASDAQ. This results in related regulation of closed-end funds under the 1934 Act and applicable stock exchange or NASDAQ requirements, including the composition and functioning of audit committees, and related disclosure in proxy statements. These listing requirements are being enhanced as mandated by the S-O Act. As publicly traded companies, closed-end funds are also subject to SEC requirements regulating selective disclosure of information, and their directors are subject to 1934 Act regulation of insider trading.

3. Shareholder Meetings

Listed closed-end funds, unlike many open-end funds, are required to hold annual meetings of shareholders. Closed-end funds listed on the New York and American Stock Exchanges and on NASDAQ must hold annual meetings of shareholders pursuant to stock exchange or NASDAQ requirements. Annual meetings of shareholders of closed-end funds provide regular forums for proposals and board nominations by shareholders. Although proxy-soliciting rules under the 1934 Act are applicable to shareholder solicitations by both open-end and closed-end funds, the requirement that closed-end funds hold annual meetings of shareholders makes these rules of much greater practical significance to closed-end funds. See Section 3.B for information as to the extent to which open-end funds must have shareholder meetings.

4. Tendency of Closed-End Fund Shares to Trade at a Discount

Like shares of other publicly traded companies, the market prices of closed-end fund shares are subject to the forces of supply and demand. Although shares of closed-end funds sometimes trade at premiums to their net asset value, they frequently trade at discounts from net asset value. The tendency of closed-end fund shares to trade at discounts has resulted in significant shareholder activism, often presenting issues for consideration by their boards of directors.

B. Senior Securities and Leverage

Unlike open-end funds, closed-end funds are permitted, within limits imposed by the 1940 Act, their organizational documents and their investment policies, to issue debt securities and preferred stock (referred to in Section 18 of the 1940 Act as "senior securities") in addition to common equity securities. Directors are responsible for determining the appropriateness of issuing senior securities and the amount from time-to-time outstanding. Directors should understand the risks and benefits of leverage and should monitor their fund's use of leverage to insure that management uses leverage in an appropriate and prudent manner.

C. Offerings of Common Equity

Closed-end funds frequently raise additional capital through the offering of common shares, generally through offerings of transferable or nontransferable rights. Section 23(b) of the 1940 Act prohibits closed-end funds from selling their common shares at below their net asset value except under limited circumstances. The exception usually relied upon is that permitting a rights offering to existing shareholders. The SEC requires the directors of closed-end funds to make a good faith determination that a rights offering will result in a net benefit to existing shareholders. This means that the directors must determine that the benefits of the rights offering to both subscribing and nonsubscribing shareholders outweigh the resulting dilution of per share net asset value and other negative effects. Benefits may include, for example, the anticipated return on investment of the proceeds, a reduction in per share expense ratio and the opportunity for shareholders to purchase shares at below net asset value. Dilution will result both from the sale of shares at below net asset value and the costs of conducting the offering, including any dealer-manager fees. Other negative effects may include a potential adverse impact on the short-term or long-term market prices of the fund's shares resulting from the market overhang or increased trading float during and after consummation of the rights offering. The offering of transferable rights gives nonsubscribing shareholders the opportunity to offset the dilutive effect of the rights offering through sale of their rights in the open market.

Although advice on the above issues should be sought from the fund's investment manager and any proposed dealer-manager for the rights offering, independent directors should understand that each has an inherent conflict of interest resulting from the prospect either of increased advisory fees or dealer-manager fees earned as a result of the offering. Independent directors, therefore, should consult with independent counsel in connection with their determination whether a rights offering will result in a net benefit to shareholders.

D. Illiquid Investments

The SEC limits investment by open-end funds in illiquid securities to 15 percent of net assets. This limitation reflects concerns relating to the need of open-end funds to maintain liquidity to meet redemptions. As closed-end funds do not have these ongoing pressures on liquidity, there is no such general limitation on closed-end funds. Substantial investment in illiquid securities by closed-end funds can, however, affect liquidity for portfolio management and other corporate purposes for any applicable asset coverage tests and for publication in the financial press. Directors should understand and monitor their fund's policies and practices with regard to investment in illiquid securities.

E. Interval Funds

An interval fund is a hybrid closed-end fund that has elected, pursuant to Rule 23c-3 under the 1940 Act, to repurchase a stated percentage of its outstanding common shares at net asset value at regular intervals, e.g., quarterly or semi-annually. Because of the ongoing obligation to repurchase their shares, regulation of leverage and liquidity of interval funds under the 1940 Act is more stringent than for other closed-end funds. The terms of any debt securities or borrowings must provide flexibility for repayment, without premium or penalty, prior to each repurchase pricing date as needed to insure compliance with the asset coverage requirements of Section 18. In addition, an interval fund's board of directors must adopt written procedures designed to insure that the fund has sufficient liquid assets to meet its periodic repurchase obligations.

F. Share Repurchases

Closed-end funds, other than interval funds, are not required to repurchase their shares unless they have undertaken to do so in connection with their initial public offering or otherwise. When shares of a closed-end fund are trading at significant discounts from their net asset value, however, boards of directors frequently have determined that share repurchases are in the best interests of the fund. Purchases at below net asset value, for example, have an antidilutive benefit to a fund by increasing the fund's per share net asset value. Share repurchases are often made through open-market purchase programs. Sometimes they are made through tender offers at net asset value or at prices representing more favorable discounts from net asset value than those available in the market.

Regulation of share repurchases under the 1940 Act is designed to insure equal treatment of shareholders. Section 23(c) of the 1940 Act permits a closed-end fund to make open-market purchases of its shares, provided that the fund has informed shareholders within the preceding six months of its intent to make such purchases, and to make tender offers on the same terms to all shareholders. Privately negotiated repurchases by closed-end funds are regulated by Rule 23c-1. This rule includes a prohibition against repurchases from affiliated persons of a fund, e.g., a holder of 5 percent or more of the fund's shares, and a requirement that the purchase price not be higher than market value or net asset value, whichever is lower.

G. SEC and Stock Exchange Regulation

The 1934 Act (as amended by the S-O Act), the New York and American Stock Exchanges and NASDAQ regulate the composition and functioning of audit committees of closed-end funds and related proxy statement disclosure. As publicly traded companies, closed-end funds are also subject to SEC Regulation FD, which prohibits certain selective disclosure of material information. Directors and officers of closed-end funds are subject to the requirements of the 1934 Act regulating insider trading.

1. Audit Committee Requirements

The New York and American Stock Exchanges and NASDAQ require the boards of directors of listed companies, including closed-end funds, to appoint audit committees, consisting of at least three members who are both independent, as defined, and "financially literate," with at least one member having accounting or financial management expertise. Members of audit committees should have a sufficient understanding of financial reporting and internal control principles to understand and consider material financial reporting and internal control issues. In addition, the stock exchanges and NASDAQ require boards of directors of listed companies to adopt audit committee charters setting forth the responsibilities of the committees. Audit committees must certify annually that they have reviewed the adequacy of their charters. The compensation, duties and powers of audit committees of closed-end funds, including the need to disclose whether at least one member is an "audit committee financial expert," as defined by the SEC, are more fully described in Section 4.B.

The proxy-soliciting rules require disclosure in a closed-end fund's proxy statement for its annual meeting of shareholders relating to the deliberations and composition of its audit committee. These rules also require inclusion in the proxy statement of a report of the audit committee stating whether it has recommended to the board of directors the inclusion of the fund's audited financial statements in its annual report to shareholders.

These 1934 Act and listing requirements impose obligations on the board of directors and the audit committee of a closed-end fund in addition to their general duties under state law. The board of directors and audit committee of a closed-end fund should consult with counsel as to the contents of the fund's audit committee charter and related disclosure in the fund's proxy statement.

2. Short-Swing Profits

Section 16(a) of the 1934 Act requires, among other things, that directors of a publicly traded company file with the SEC reports as to their ownership of the company's equity securities. Section 16(b) provides generally that "short-swing" profits (i.e., profits on any purchase and sale of the company's securities within six months) realized by any such directors are recoverable by the company. Under Section 16, as made applicable to directors of closed-end funds by Section 30(h) of the 1940 Act, directors of a closed-end fund are required to disclose, in accordance with applicable SEC filing requirements, their holdings of, and transactions in, all securities of the fund (other than short-term paper) beneficially owned by them. A director's failure to make these filings on a timely basis must be publicly disclosed in the fund's proxy statement for its annual meeting of shareholders. The S-O Act has greatly accelerated the reporting deadline for trades by directors to two business days after the trade date.

3. Insider Trading

Directors of closed-end funds, like directors of other publicly traded companies, are prohibited from (i) purchasing or selling securities when they possess material, nonpublic information about the fund, (ii) "tipping" or disclosing such information to others who may use it in trading, and (iii) giving others recommendations to buy or sell while in possession of such information. Information is material if there is a substantial likelihood that a reasonable investor would consider it important in deciding whether to buy, sell or hold a security. Some believe that information may be considered material if, upon disclosure, it would likely affect the stock price. If there is any doubt whether information is material, legal guidance should be sought or, as a practical alternative, the information should be treated as material. Closed-end fund directors may become privy to nonpublic information, which may be material, such as information pertaining to a prospective tender offer or rights offering by the fund, a change in the fund's historical dividend rate or the impact on the fund of the bankruptcy of the issuer of one of its significant portfolio holdings.

Purchasing or selling by a director of a closed-end fund of a security based upon material, nonpublic information about the fund or merely passing the information on to someone else who acts on that information is illegal. Insider trading by a director may result in criminal prosecution, disgorgement of profits, fines and other sanctions in actions instituted by the SEC. Consequently, directors should exercise caution in their own trading activities and in discussing with others the information they learn in the course of performing their duties. Similarly, directors should exercise caution so that information learned through their service as officers or directors of public companies is not improperly communicated to the fund and its affiliates.

H. Corporate Governance and the Discount

The tendency of closed-end fund shares to trade at a discount has resulted in shareholder activism seeking to cause boards of directors of closed-end funds to take action to reduce or eliminate the discounts. Actions proposed by shareholders have included open-ending, share repurchase programs and liquidation. Proxy contests to replace incumbent directors have also been waged. Directors should understand the extent of their duties in this regard under both state corporate law and the federal proxy-soliciting rules.

1. Duties and Powers of Directors

The SEC requires prominent disclosure in prospectuses for offerings of closed-end fund shares of the tendency of closed-end fund shares to trade at a discount from their net asset value. In addition, underwriters for many of these offerings have required closed-end funds to adopt various policies, which may be embodied in charter provisions, to address investors' concerns about the discount. These have included undertakings to consider discretionary actions, such as open-market share repurchases or tender offers, and mandatory actions, such as obligations to make tender offers or put an open-ending vote to shareholders if shares trade for specified periods at stated discount levels.

The market value of a corporation's common stock is of obvious importance to shareholders and a legitimate concern of the board of directors. In the exercise of their duties, it is proper for directors of a closed-end fund to consider the benefits and costs to the fund of addressing the discount and to take action reasonably believed by them to be in the best interests of the fund. Directors' duties to direct the management of the business and affairs of the fund do not, however, necessarily include any obligation to deal with the market price of a fund's common shares. Directors acting within applicable standards of conduct under state law do not ordinarily breach their duties in failing to take action to address the discount. Directors may, however, have special duties in this regard as a result of obligations undertaken in connection with a closed-end fund's initial public offering or otherwise.

Shareholders do not have the right under general principles of corporate law to take direct corporate action relating to the business and affairs of a corporation but must act through the board of directors. The oversight responsibility of the directors is designed to insure that management is carried out in the interests of the fund and not the variable and conflicting interests of a changing shareholder base. For this reason, shareholder proposals to address the discount, such as proposals for open-ending or liquidation, typically must be cast as recommendations to the board of directors to take the specified actions. Although directors should give careful consideration to any advisory shareholder proposal approved by shareholders, their duty to direct the management of the business and affairs of the fund in the overall interests of the fund remains paramount. The recourse of shareholders dissatisfied with the governance of directors is to replace those directors through a proxy contest.

2. Actions to Address the Discount

Boards of directors of a closed-end fund may choose to take action to address discount levels at which shares of the fund are trading if they reasonably believe that they are acting in the best interests of the fund. Actions taken by boards of directors of closed-end funds include measures ranging from share repurchases to open-ending.

Share repurchases can be effected through open-market purchases or tender offers for a limited percentage of a fund's outstanding shares. Although share repurchases may have a temporary favorable impact on discount levels, there is no evidence demonstrating that they have any long-term effect. There may, however, be other benefits to the fund, such as the anti-dilutive benefit of repurchasing shares at prices below net asset value.

Open-ending, by conversion or by merger into an open-end fund, is the only measure that permits continued operations while definitively eliminating the discount. Open-ending, however, is a fundamental change in structure with major effects that must be carefully considered by boards of directors. The major consequences of open-ending have been immediate, massive redemptions of shares, frequently of more than 50 percent of outstanding shares, and the need for the capability to distribute fund shares continuously to offset both immediate and ongoing redemptions. Another important consideration is whether the existing portfolio holdings of the fund will comply with the portfolio liquidity standards applicable to open-end funds. Tax consequences and increased per-share operating expenses must also be considered. Some of these consequences may be ameliorated if open-ending is accomplished through merger into an open-end fund with similar investment objectives.

Other measures to address the discount include the election of interval fund status and the adoption of a managed distribution policy. The latter attempts to increase market demand for a closed-end fund's shares through the establishment of an attractive monthly, quarterly or other periodic distribution rate, e.g., 10 percent per annum, regardless of actual investment income or realized gains. If earnings are insufficient, a portion of distributions will consist of a return of capital.

All measures to address the discount have advantages and disadvantages, which must be considered in light of each fund's particular circumstances and applicable legal and regulatory requirements. Boards of directors of closed-end funds should consult with counsel, their fund's investment manager and other appropriate advisers before taking action to address the discount.

3. Board Governance Measures

Directors may elect to adopt various measures designed to enhance their power to direct the management of their fund in accordance with the division of power under state law between directors and shareholders. These measures may include (i) establishing a classified board, i.e., a board with staggered terms; (ii) providing in the fund's charter provisions for a supermajority vote to effect extraordinary actions such as open-ending, liquidation or mergers; (iii) adopting an advanced-notice bylaw requiring minimum advanced notice of shareholder proposals or board nominations; (iv) establishing qualification requirements for nominees for election as directors; and (v) vesting exclusive power to amend bylaws in the board of directors. The availability of these and other measures will depend upon applicable state law, and implementation of certain measures after a fund's initial public offering may require a vote of shareholders. In their deliberations concerning the adoption and implementation of these provisions, directors must adhere to state law standards of conduct and have a reasonable belief that they are acting in the best interests of the fund.

4. Federal Proxy Rules

Stock exchange and NASDAQ listing requirements impose an obligation on closed-end funds to hold annual meetings of shareholders even when not required under applicable state law. Shareholders are therefore able to make proposals or nominate directors each year. Federal law requires publicly owned companies, including investment companies, that solicit proxies for shareholder votes on election of directors or other matters to furnish each shareholder with a proxy statement, which must be filed with, and may be reviewed by, the SEC. Shareholders may file their own proxy statements to solicit proxies for their proposals and must do so to solicit proxies for their nominees for the board of directors.

Shareholders frequently opt, however, to take advantage of Rule 14a-8 of the federal proxy rules, which permits timely proposals by qualified shareholders to be included in a fund's proxy statement for its annual meeting of shareholders. The rule also provides various grounds on which shareholder proposals may be excluded from the fund's proxy statement. The SEC staff is reviewing the proxy rules relating to the nomination and election of directors, including proposals that would give shareholders greater access to the nomination process.

It is good practice for directors to review a proxy statement before it is filed with the SEC or disseminated to shareholders, particularly if nonroutine matters or shareholder proposals are included. Directors also should determine the fund's position with respect to shareholder proposals or board nominees. It is proper for directors to authorize a fund to incur costs to oppose shareholder proposals or nominees for the board of directors if they reasonably believe they are acting in the bests interests of the fund.

SECTION **14**

Responsibilities and Duties of Fund Directors under State Law

A. General Responsibilities

Fund directors, like directors of operating companies, have two basic functions under state law: decision-making and oversight. The decision-making function includes both matters as to which the law requires board action—e.g., election of officers, dividend authorization, approval of charter amendments and mergers—and other matters where board approval is good corporate practice. The oversight function does not, in general, involve specifically required decisions or approvals but rather concerns periodic attention to corporate systems and controls, policy issues and other recurring matters as well as discrete attention to matters suggesting a need for inquiry. In pursuit of both their decision-making and oversight activities, corporate directors have, individually or collectively, various duties, responsibilities and rights, which are more fully described below.

Directors of funds have responsibility for such matters as (i) reviewing and approving fundamental operating, financial and corporate governance policies; (ii) evaluating the manager's performance and taking appropriate action, including nonrenewal or removal when warranted; (iii) reviewing and approving investment management fees; and (iv) reviewing procedures for providing financial and operational information to the board. In addition, directors are subject to provisions of state law (as well as certain overlapping federal provisions) that deal with such matters as (i) the size of the board and the procedure for changing size; (ii) the method for selecting directors and filling vacancies; (iii) operation of committees of the board; (iv) issuance of shares;

(v) authorization of dividends; (vi) calling of regular or special meetings of shareholders; (vii) appointment of officers and agents; and (viii) review of major transactions. The extent of this review function varies depending upon the nature and importance of the matter in question.

A director generally is entitled to rely on reports, opinions, information, and statements (including financial statements and other financial data) presented by the fund's officers or employees, its investment adviser, administrator or distributor so long as the director reasonably believes the presenter to be reliable and competent in the matters presented. A director may similarly rely upon legal counsel, independent public accountants, and other persons as to matters that the director reasonably believes to be within their professional or expert competence. A director may also rely on a board committee on which the director does not serve as to a matter within its power if the director reasonably believes that the committee merits confidence.

B. Duty of Loyalty and Duty of Care

The duties of directors under state law are generally characterized as a duty of loyalty and a duty of care.

The duty of loyalty requires a director to exercise his or her powers in the interests of the fund and not in the director's own interest or in the interest of another person or organization. Simply put, directors should not use their position for personal profit, gain or other personal advantage. Where a director has a personal interest in a transaction involving the fund, the director should take particular precautions to avoid improper self-dealing and to satisfy the applicable legal requirements. Most state corporation statutes, as well as the law applicable to business trusts, prescribe conditions or procedures for authorization, approval or ratification of interested director transactions in order to insulate such transactions from being void.

In Maryland and Delaware, where many funds are organized, and in states that have adopted the Model Business Corporation Act (the "Model Act"), a director who acts in good faith, with the care an ordinarily prudent person in a like position would exercise under similar circumstances and in a manner the director reasonably believes to be in the best interests of the fund as a continuing entity has met his or her duty of care to the fund. Compliance with the duty of care under state law is based upon diligence applied to the ordinary and extraordinary needs of the fund, including regular attendance and participation in board and committee meetings, obtaining and reviewing adequate information on which to base decisions, avoiding undue haste and making appropriate inquiries as required under particular circumstances. The director should share with other directors, as appropriate, his or her advice and views based upon business experience and public and professional relationships.

Courts have not often sustained damage awards against directors for breach of the duty of care but have instead indicated that they will impose liability for breach of this duty only in cases of obvious or prolonged failure to participate diligently and to exercise oversight or supervision. However, recent decisions have re-emphasized the need for directors to take an active, rather than a passive, role in meeting their duty of care if liability is to be avoided.

In addition to liability for breach of the duties of care or loyalty, state law may also impose liability on directors for specific actions, such as authorizing unlawful dividends or other distributions or authorizing violations of the fund's governing instrument. Directors may also be subject to personal liability under other state and federal laws. Good faith and careful monitoring of management programs directed toward corporate legal compliance should provide substantial safeguards against personal liability.

In Delaware, the courts have, in recent years, also spoken of another aspect of a director's duty—fiduciary duty of disclosure, or candor, which is said to flow from both the duties of care and loyalty. This emerging concept encompasses the idea that directors of a corporation should furnish shareholders with all material relevant information known to the directors when the directors present the shareholders with a voting or investment decision. This duty may also extend to the related concept that directors should not mislead or misinform shareholders about the affairs of the corporation.

C. The Business Judgment Rule

If directors' decisions are challenged in court by a claimant asserting deficient conduct, judicial review of the matter will normally be governed by the business judgment rule. The business judgment rule, well-established in case law, protects a disinterested director from personal liability to the corporation and its shareholders, even though a corporate action approved by the director turns out to be unwise or unsuccessful. The business judgment rule presumes that, in making a business decision, directors acted in good faith and in the honest belief that the action taken was in the best interests of the corporation.

Unlike the standards of conduct encompassed in the duties of care and loyalty, the business judgment rule is not a description of a duty or standard used to determine whether a breach of duty has occurred. It is instead a standard of judicial review used in analyzing director conduct to determine whether a board decision can be successfully challenged or a director should be held personally liable. In suits brought against directors by shareholders acting for themselves or derivatively on behalf of the corporation, the court will look only to determine whether the directors—at least those directors making the decision—were disinterested in the matter (i.e., did not have conflicting personal interests), appropriately informed themselves before deciding and acted with a good faith belief that the decision was in the best interests of the corporation.

Personal liability of directors may be limited or offset by indemnification or insurance as discussed in Section 15.

SECTION **15**

Liability Limitation, Indemnification and Insurance

Directors may incur personal liability and expenses for claims of breach of their duties of care and loyalty to the fund, as well as for claims of failure to satisfy their obligations under the federal securities laws or other applicable laws. A director who is sued for breach of duty or for another violation of law may be exculpated from liability under state law by a provision in the fund's charter, may be entitled to indemnification and advance of expenses from the fund pursuant to its charter, by-laws or an indemnification contract between the fund and its directors, and may be covered by a directors' and officers' liability insurance policy.

Both the SEC and the ICI best practices report have strongly recommended that a fund board obtain directors' and officers' liability insurance coverage and/or indemnification from the fund that is adequate to ensure the independence and effectiveness of the fund's independent directors.

A. Limitation of Liability

A majority of the state corporation laws, the Model Act and business trust law permit a fund to include in its charter a provision limiting directors' personal liability to the fund and its shareholders for money damages for breaches of the duty of care. Typically, availability of this protection depends upon additional factors, such as whether the director has engaged in conduct specifically excepted from the statute. Further, liability limitation does not extend to liability to third parties, claims for nonmonetary or equitable relief or, in particular, violations of the federal securities laws.

In addition to state law limitations on liability limitation, the 1940 Act also restricts a fund's ability to protect or attempt to protect a director from liability to the fund or its shareholders for certain disabling conduct (willful misfeasance, bad faith, gross negligence or reckless disregard of duties). Thus, a fund cannot take advantage of state laws that permit the exculpation of liability for misconduct that goes beyond simple negligence.

B. Indemnification

Most state corporation statutes specify the circumstances in which the corporation is permitted or is required to indemnify its directors against liability and related reasonable expenses incurred in connection with their service as directors of the corporation. Funds often agree to indemnify directors to the fullest extent permitted by law against liability and reasonable expenses incurred as a result of their service as directors. The permissible indemnification for fund directors depends upon a fund's jurisdiction and form of organization and the fund's policies. Fund directors and their counsel should review the specific indemnification provisions applicable to the fund with particular regard to whether indemnification is mandatory or permissible and the types of proceedings (e.g., civil, criminal or administrative), conduct and time frame covered (e.g., whether protection with respect to prior conduct continues after a director retires).

State law places certain limits on indemnification. Under the Model Act, a director may be indemnified by a corporation when he or she has acted in good faith and with a reasonable belief that his or her conduct was in the best interests of the corporation. In the case of criminal proceedings, the director must also have had no reasonable cause to believe his or her conduct was unlawful. The Model Act also permits a corporation to provide in its charter for broader indemnification, subject to certain limitations. Moreover, as noted, the 1940 Act prohibits a fund from indemnifying its directors for liability to the fund or its shareholders arising from the directors' willful misfeasance, bad faith, gross negligence or reckless disregard of duties. The SEC staff interprets this provision to require a fund to use "reasonable and fair means" to determine whether the disabling conduct exists. According to the staff, "reasonable and fair means" would include (i) a final decision by a court or other body on the merits, (ii) a reasonable determination based upon a review of the facts by a vote of a majority of the disinterested directors not involved in the proceeding, or (iii) such a reasonable determination by an independent legal counsel in a written opinion. The SEC also takes the position that indemnification for liabilities arising under the 1933 Act "is against public policy."

C. Advance for Expenses

Most state corporation statutes specify the circumstances in which corporations may advance funds to directors to pay or reimburse reasonable expenses incurred by them in defense of a matter prior to the final disposition of the proceedings and before final determination of their right to indemnification for those expenses. The directors generally must provide the corporation with a written undertaking that any funds advanced by the corporation will be repaid if it is ultimately determined that they are not entitled to indemnification. In addition, the SEC staff takes the position that prior to an advance, one of the following must occur: (i) the director must give security for the advance; (ii) the fund must have insurance against losses arising from lawful advances; or (iii) the disinterested nonparty directors, or independent legal counsel in a written opinion, must determine that the director would be entitled to indemnification. In making a determination that an independent director would be entitled to indemnification (and, therefore, entitled to an advancement of expenses), the SEC staff has taken the position that the disinterested nonparty directors, or independent legal counsel, may rebuttably presume that such an independent director did not engage in disabling conduct. In addition, state law often requires the director to sign a good faith affirmation that the director meets the applicable standard for indemnification.

D. Insurance Issues

Although not required by law, many funds purchase and maintain directors' and officers'/errors and omissions liability insurance (D&O/E&O) for their directors. Not all D&O/E&O policies are the same. Typically, a D&O/E&O policy will protect a fund and its directors, officers and employees from certain liabilities and expenses that may arise from actions taken or not taken by such persons in the conduct of their duties. Coverage, terms and conditions may vary significantly, depending upon the policy and the insurer. The key areas of difference among D&O/E&O policies include (i) the claims covered (e.g., whether administrative actions brought by the government are covered); (ii) the types of wrongful acts covered (e.g., intentional or negligent); (ii) at what point the insurer will pay (before or after expenses are incurred); (iv) whether defense costs will be advanced and, if so, whether costs of defending an investigation are covered or only the costs of defending a complaint; and (v) when notice of a claim must be given. For noninvestment companies, D&O/E&O policies often provide coverage, subject to certain limitations, beyond that which is indemnifiable, e.g., disabling conduct and securities law violations.

Funds typically purchase D&O/E&O policies jointly with other funds in their complex, as well as with the funds' adviser and/or underwriter. Some portion of the coverage under a joint policy may be reserved exclusively for the directors and not available to the other insured. Joint coverage is permitted under the 1940 Act if the board of directors of each covered fund makes certain determinations, and the independent directors and their counsel meet the minimum independence requirements set forth in the SEC corporate governance standards discussed in Section 3. The primary advantage of a joint policy is that it usually enables all parties to obtain a greater amount of overall coverage at a relatively lower premium. In determining the appropriate amount of total coverage under a joint policy, however, directors should consider the risk that the limits of the policy may be exhausted by another insured. In addition, a joint policy requires the directors to allocate the premium and/or recoveries first between the funds and the adviser/underwriter and, second, between each of the funds. Often, fund boards will seek an estimate from the insurer of the costs of separate policies for the funds versus a joint policy along with a recommended premium split. Although the premium split may vary widely among fund complexes, typically the insurer will apply a higher percentage to the adviser/underwriter (e.g., 60 percent/40 percent).

The D&O/E&O policy also allows the fund to protect itself against its potential indemnification expenses, as well as offer further protection to directors against potential defense costs and liabilities that may result from their service to the fund. The availability of insurance may be important if, for instance, the fund is insolvent or is unwilling to indemnify former directors, or if state or federal law limits indemnification or advancement of expenses. Where a fund is unable, for whatever reason, to purchase adequate D&O/E&O coverage, the independent directors may consider purchasing insurance covering just the independent directors or a director may consider purchasing insurance individually.

Glossary

Administrator: Entity that provides administrative but not investment advisory services to a fund.
Advisers Act: The Investment Advisers Act of 1940, as amended, which regulates investment advisers to funds.
Affiliated Persons: Categories of persons specified in Section 2(a)(3) of the 1940 Act having specific degrees of affiliation with the other entity, such as owning 5 percent or more of the voting securities of such entity (or vice versa), having control or common control relationships or acting as an officer, director or employee of the other entity.
Amortized Cost Method of Valuation: A method of valuation for money market funds to facilitate the maintenance of a constant net asset value permitted by Rule 2a-7, pursuant to which portfolio securities are valued at the fund's cost adjusted for amortization of premium or discount rather than at current market value.
Audit Committee: A committee consisting of independent directors from the board of directors which has extensive responsibilities with respect to the retention of the fund's auditors and the review of the fund's financial statements and other finance-related matters.
Bank-Related Fund: A fund that is managed by a bank or sold through bank distribution channels and subject to the banking laws.
Closed-End Fund: A fund whose shares are nonredeemable and whose shares trade in the secondary market at prices that are not tied to net asset value.
Codes of Ethics: The rules under the 1940 Act require a code of ethics that funds, investment advisers and distributors must adopt, which is designed to prevent persons with access to information—as to fund portfolio security activities—from engaging in fraudulent, deceptive or manipulative trading practices. The S-O Act requires disclosure as to whether funds, their advisers and distributors have adopted a code of

ethics that covers their CEO and principal financial officers. The two codes may be integrated.

Custody Arrangements: The manner in which the assets of a fund are held. The 1940 Act requires that the securities of a fund be maintained in the custody of a qualified custodian. There are special provisions related to custody with custodians and security depositories of foreign securities in foreign countries.

Distributor: The entity responsible for selling the shares of the mutual fund, which may, in turn, contract with brokers/dealers and other intermediaries for the sale of fund shares to the public. The distributor is referred to in the 1940 Act as the "principal underwriter." The distribution arrangements of a mutual fund are subject to regulation under the 1940 Act and the sales practices are subject to regulation by the NASD.

Diversified: A diversified fund is limited by the 1940 Act as to the proportion of its assets that it may invest in securities of a single issuer. Funds must elect, under the 1940 Act, to be classified as a diversified or nondiversified fund.

Exchange-Traded Funds: Hybrid investment companies traded on a stock exchange that contain features of open-end and closed-end funds.

Expense Ratio: Ratio, usually expressed as a percentage, that compares annual fund expenses for management fee and other operating expenses to average net asset value of the outstanding shares during the year.

Fidelity Bond: The bond that each fund must maintain against larceny or embezzlement. The form and amount of the bond are subject to 1940 Act regulation.

Financial Expert: A term defined in the S-O Act to denote members of the audit committee who have financial expertise.

Fund: See "Investment Company."

Fund of Funds: An investment company organized to invest in other investment companies.

Gramm-Leach-Bliley Act: The legislation enacted in 1999 that eliminated most of the Glass-Steagall Act barriers that restricted the extent to which banks can engage in the fund business.

Hedge Funds: See "Private Investment Companies."

Independent Director: A fund director who is not an "interested person" as defined in Section 2(a)(19) of the 1940 Act. Members of the audit committee are subject to further independence requirements under the S-O Act.

Interested Persons: Any one of several categories of persons specified in Section 2(a)(19) of the 1940 Act having interests potentially in conflict with the fund. The "interested person" category is broader than the "affiliated person" category. Generally, at least 40 percent of the board of directors of a fund must consist of directors who are not interested persons of the fund.
Interval Fund: Hybrid closed-end fund that is permitted to make periodic mandatory repurchase offers without having to comply with the tender offer rules.
Investment Adviser: The entity responsible for the portfolio management and typically all matters necessary for the operation of the fund. The investment adviser may be referred to as the adviser, manager, investment manager or some other variation thereof. The management arrangements may be split between the adviser and an administrator or a sub-adviser (which assumes specified advisor responsibilities). The management arrangements are regulated under the 1940 Act and the activities of investment advisers and sub-advisers are subject to regulation under the Advisers Act.
Investment Company: An entity that invests in securities and sells its shares to the public is registered under the 1940 Act and is subject to regulation thereunder. Certain investment companies, such as those offered privately with fewer than 100 security holders, those offered only to investors meeting certain qualifications ("private investment companies" or "hedge funds") or those with funds sold to foreign investors ("offshore funds"), are exempt from 1940 Act registration.
ICI: The Investment Company Institute, which is the national association of the American investment company industry.
ICI Best Practices Report: The Investment Company Institute–sponsored "best practices report," developed by an advisory group and identifying a variety of corporate governance practices beyond those required by law.
Listing Requirements: The listing requirements for closed-end funds with securities listed on a stock exchange or association. Certain requirements of the S-O Act are implemented through the listing requirements of the national securities exchanges and NASDAQ. Although not applicable to open-end funds, the listing requirements may serve as a "best practices" guide for open-end funds.
Load Fund: A fund that imposes a sales charge in connection with the sale of its shares.
Manager: See "Investment Adviser."

Master-Feeder Fund: Two-tier fund structure involving an underlying fund ("master fund") from which emanates any number of first-tier funds ("feeder funds") having as their sole investment an investment in the underlying SEC-registered master fund. The various feeder funds need not necessarily be 1940 Act entities and may have different distribution arrangements.

Money Market Fund: Fund that invests in short-term money market instruments and offers investors relative safety of principal, a high degree of liquidity and a wide range of shareholder services (including check-writing) and that seeks to maintain a stable net asset value (usually $1.00 per share). Such funds are sometimes referred to as money funds. The shares of the money fund may either be taxable ("taxable money fund") or exempt from federal taxation ("tax-free money fund"), depending primarily upon whether the portfolio money market securities are taxable or tax-exempt.

Multiple-Class Fund: A mutual fund that issues separate classes of securities, each with a different distribution arrangement, but each representing interests in the same portfolio of securities.

Mutual Fund: A term not defined in the 1940 Act that is commonly used to refer to an open-end fund.

NASD: The National Association of Securities Dealers, Inc. is a self-regulatory organization of almost all securities firms and is subject to SEC jurisdiction and review. The NASD regulates, among other things, the sales practices of broker/dealers selling shares of funds.

Net Asset Value Per Share: The price upon which the purchase and redemption price of shares of open-end funds is derived. The net asset value per share is computed by dividing the sum of the value of the securities held by the fund plus any cash or other assets (including accrued interest and dividends receivable) less all liabilities (including accrued expenses) by the total number of shares outstanding at such time.

1933 Act: The Securities Act of 1933, as amended, which is a disclosure statute designed to ensure that investors are provided with full and fair disclosure of material information in connection with the offering and sale of fund shares.

1934 Act: The Securities Exchange Act of 1934, as amended, which regulates the securities markets and broker-dealers as well as imposing ongoing reporting and proxy requirements on public companies. Many of the provisions of the S-O Act are set forth in the 1934 Act.

1940 Act: The Investment Company Act of 1940, as amended, which contains comprehensive provisions regulating investment companies registered thereunder.

No-Load Fund: A fund that sells its shares at net asset value without any sales charge.

Non-Diversified: See "Diversified."

Open-End Fund: A fund that issues shares redeemable at net asset value at any time at the option of the shareholder and typically engages in a continuous offering of its shares. Open-end funds are commonly referred to as "mutual funds."

Penny-Rounding Method of Pricing: A method of pricing for money market funds to facilitate the maintenance of a constant net asset value permitted by Rule 2a-7 in which the current net asset value is rounded to the nearest one percent.

Pricing: The daily process of determining the price at which open-end fund shares are sold and redeemed, which is based upon the net asset value of the shares.

Principal Underwriter: The term used in the 1940 Act to denote the person principally responsible for selling the shares of the fund. The principal underwriter is frequently referred to as the "distributor."

Private Investment Companies: Pooled investment entities exempt from the registration and reporting requirements of the 1940 Act. See "Investment Company."

Redemption: The requirement that open-end funds must redeem shares each business day at the redemption price per share, which is based upon the net asset value per share next determined after receipt of the notice of redemption from the shareholder. The manner in which redemptions are handled is regulated under the 1940 Act.

Regulated Investment Company: The tax term denoting a fund that qualifies for the special flow-through tax treatment afforded under subsection M of the Internal Revenue Code. Funds that so qualify are entitled to deduct from their taxable income the part of the income distributed to shareholders.

Rule 12b-1 Plan: A distribution plan organized pursuant to the requirements of Rule 12b-1 under the 1940 Act, which specifies conditions pursuant to which a fund may use its own assets for marketing or promotional purposes in the sale of fund shares.

Rule 2a-7: The rule under the 1940 Act that contains comprehensive provisions regulating funds that hold themselves out as money market funds. Among other things, Rule 2a-7 requires money market funds to satisfy detailed requirements as to portfolio quality, maturity and diversification.

Sales Charges: Charges imposed in connection with the sale of mutual fund shares, which can be imposed at the time of sale (a front-end load) or on a deferred basis pursuant to a Rule 12b-1 plan.

The S-O Act: The Sarbanes-Oxley Act of 2002, which contains sweeping reforms as to the manner in which funds are regulated.

SEC: The Securities and Exchange Commission. The federal regulatory agency responsible for administering the federal securities laws, including the 1940 Act. The powers of the SEC include the interpretation, supervision and enforcement of the 1940 Act. The SEC staff regularly conducts detailed inspections of funds and investment advisers.

SEC Governance Standards: A special set of governance standards that apply to funds that have adopted Rule 12b-1 plans, issue multiple classes of shares or rely upon widely used SEC-exemptive rules to engage in certain types of transactions with affiliates. The exemptive rules include a number of rules that ease the prohibitions on portfolio and other transactions involving affiliates.

Series Fund: A fund that has multiple portfolios of securities, each of which is in effect a separate fund typically with separate investment objections and policies.

Sponsor: The entity that causes the organization of the investment company referred to in the 1940 Act as the "promoter."

Subsection M: A subsection of the Internal Revenue Code containing the provisions that establish the requirements for taxation as a regulated investment company. See "Regulated Investment Company."

Unit Investment Trust: A trust registered under the 1940 Act that has a fixed portfolio of securities and issues redeemable securities. A UIT does not have a board of directors.

The USA Patriot Act: The USA Patriot Act of 2001, which requires funds to adopt anti–money laundering programs.

Bibliography

Many of the following authorities are specific to fund directors; others relate to corporate directors generally. All are potentially useful to fund directors and their counsel.

Books

JEREMY BACON, CORPORATE BOARDS AND CORPORATE GOVERNANCE (1993).

R. FRANKLIN BALOTTI & JESSE A. FINKELSTEIN, THE DELAWARE LAW OF CORPORATIONS AND OTHER BUSINESS ORGANIZATIONS ch. 4 (Directors and Officers) (Aspen Law & Business Supp. 2000).

DENNIS BLOCK, NANCY BARTON & STEPHEN RADIN, THE BUSINESS JUDGMENT RULE: FIDUCIARY DUTIES OF CORPORATE DIRECTORS (5th ed. 1998).

WILLIAM G. BOWEN, INSIDE THE BOARDROOM: GOVERNANCE BY DIRECTORS AND TRUSTEES (1994).

TAMAR FRANKEL, THE REGULATION OF MONEY MANAGERS ch. VIII (1978).

JAMES J. HANKS, JR., MARYLAND CORPORATION LAW ch. 6 (Directors and Officers) (Aspen Publishers Supp. 2002).

INVESTMENT COMPANY INSTITUTE, REPORT OF THE ADVISORY GROUP ON BEST PRACTICES FOR FUND DIRECTORS. ENHANCING A CULTURE OF INDEPENDENCE AND EFFECTIVENESS (June 24, 1999), *available at* http://www.ici.org/pdf/rpt best practices.pdf.

INVESTMENT COMPANY INSTITUTE, GLOBAL CORPORATE GOVERNANCE ISSUES FOR MUTUAL FUNDS (2000), *available at* http://www.ici.org.

Jay W. Lorsch & Elizabeth MacIver, Pawns or Potentates: The Reality of America's Corporate Boards (1989).

Management Practice, Inc., Anthology of MPI Bulletins for Mutual Fund Directors and Their Counsel (2000).

Robert A.G. Monks & Nell Minow, Watching the Watchers: Corporate Governance for the 21st Century (Blackwell 1996).

National Association of Corporate Directors, Report of the Blue Ribbon Commission on Director Compensation (1995).

National Association of Corporate Directors, Report of Blue Ribbon Commission on Executive Compensation: Guidelines for Corporate Directors (1993).

Robert A. Robertson, Fund Governance: Legal Duties of Investment Company Directors (Law Journal Press, Supp. 2003).

United States General Accounting Office, Report on Mutual Fund Fees, Additional Disclosure Could Encourage Price Competition (GAO/GGD-00-126, June 2000).

United States Securities & Exchange Commission, Division of Investment Management, Protecting Investors: A Half Century of Investment Company Regulation ch. 7 (1992).

United States Securities & Exchange Commission, Division of Investment Management, Report on Mutual Fund Fee and Expenses (Dec. 2000).

Articles

William T. Allen, *Defining the Role of Outside Directors in an Age of Global Competition, in* Corp. Governance Today and Tomorrow (1992).

Diane E. Ambler, *Roundtable on the Role of Independent Investment Company Directors: Issues for Independent Directors of Bank-Related Funds, Variable Insurance Product Funds, and Closed-End Funds,* 55 Bus. Law. 205 (1999).

Thomas Andrews, *Termination of Section 36(b) Actions by Mutual Fund Directors: Are the Watchdogs Still The Shareholders' Best Friends?,* 50 Fordham L. Rev. 720 (1982).

R. Franklin Balotti & James J. Hanks, Jr., *Rejudging the Business Judgment Rule*, 48 BUS. LAW. 1337 (1993).

Jay G. Baris, *The New Fund Governance Standards*, 34 THE REV. SECURITIES & COMMODITIES REGULATION 135 (June 27, 2001).

Dennis Block, Michael J. Maimone & Stephen B. Ross, *The Duty of Loyalty and the Evolution of the Scope of Judicial Review*, 59 BROOKLYN L. REV. (1993).

Douglas M. Branson, *Intracorporate Process and the Avoidance of Director Liability*, 24 WAKE FOREST L. REV. (1989).

Gregory Bressler, *Concurrent Representation of the Disinterested Directors and Investment Manager of a Mutual Fund*, INV. LAW. 10 (1996).

Victor Brudney, *The Independent Director—Heavenly City or Potemkin Village?*, 95 HARV. L. REV. 597 (1982).

Business Roundtable, *Corporate Governance and American Competitiveness*, 46 BUS. LAW. 241 (1990).

Woodrow W. Campbell, *Responsibility of Mutual Fund Directors for Prospectuses, SIAs and Advertising, Investment Companies: The Changing Role of Independent Directors*, C841 ALI-ABA 213 (April 23, 1993).

Matthew Chambers, *Modernization of the Investment Company Act of 1940*, 35 HOW. L.J. 305 (1992).

David J. Carter, *Mutual Fund Boards and Shareholder Action*, 3 VILL. J.L. & INV. MGMT. 6 (2001).

Gary O. Cohen, *Disclosure of Directors' Basis for Approving Investment Advisory Contracts*, 9 INV. LAW. 1 (2002).

Comment, *Duties of the Independent Director in Open-End Mutual Funds*, 70 MICH. L. REV. 696 (1972).

Paul H. Dykstra & Paulita Pike-Bokhari, *The Yacktman Battle: Manager Bites Watchdogs*, 5 INV. LAW. 11/12 (Nov./Dec. 1998).

Meyer Eisenberg & Dennis Lehr, *An Aspect of the Emerging 'Federal Corporation Law': Directorial Responsibility Under the Investment Company Act of 1940*, 20 RUTGERS L. REV. (1966).

John P. Freeman & Stewart L. Brown, *Mutual Fund Advisory Fees: The Cost of Conflicts of Interest*, 26 J. CORP. L. 609 (2001).

Stanley J. Friedman, *Investment Advisory Agreements: Due Diligence and Approval Requirements, Including Board Procedures; Role of Outside Directors*, Role of Outside Directors, C550 ALI-ABA 1 (1990).

Stanley J. Friedman, *The Role of Outside Directors in Negotiating Investment Company Advisory Agreements*, 24 REV. SEC. & COMMOD. REG. 49 (1991).

Stanley Friedman & Ellen Metzger, *Liabilities of Investment Companies*, 17 REV. SEC. REG. 973 (1984).

Joel Goldberg, *Disinterested Directors, Individual Directors and Investment Company Act of 1940*, 3 LOY. U. CHI. L.J. 565 (1978).

Lawrence Greene, *Fiduciary Standards of Conduct Under the Investment Company Act of 1940*, 28 GEO. WASH. L. REV. 266 (1959).

Jeffrey J. Haas & Steven R. Howard. *The Heartland Funds' Receivership and its Implications for Independent Mutual Fund Directors*, 52 EMORY L. J. 153 (2002).

James J. Hanks, Jr., *Evaluating Recent State Legislation on Director and Officer Liability Limitation and Indemnification*, 43 BUS. LAW. 1207 (1988).

Charles Hansen, *The Duty of Care, the Business Judgment Rule, and the American Law Institute Corporate Governance Project*, 48 BUS. LAW. 1355 (1993).

Joseph Hinsey IV, *Business Judgment and the American Law Institute's Corporate Governance Project: The Rule, the Doctrine, and the Reality*, 52 GEO. WASH. L. REV. 609 (1984).

Joseph Hinsey IV, *The Committee System and the Role of Outside Directors, in* The Evolving Role of Outside Directors (1993).

Stephen R. Howard, et al., *Fund Governance* [Mutual Fund Regulation in the Next Millennium: Symposium, Panel Discussion], 44 N.Y.L. SCH. L. REV. 431 (2001).

Alfred Jaretzki, *Duties and Responsibilities of Directors of Mutual Funds*, 29 L. & CONTEMP. PROB. 777 (1964).

Sheldon A. Jones, *Practical Tips for the New Mutual Fund Director in the Post-Enron World*, 9 INV. LAW. 1 (2002).

Sheldon Jones, Laura Moret, & James Storey, *The Massachusetts Business Trust and Registered Investment Companies*, 13 DEL. J. CORP. L. 421 (1988).

Joseph Krupsky, *The Role of Investment Company Directors*, 32 BUS. LAW. 1733 (1977).

Arthur Levitt, Chairman, U.S. Securities & Exchange Commission, *Mutual Fund Directors as Investor Advocates*, Remarks at the Second Annual Symposium for Mutual Fund Trustees and Directors (April 11, 1995).

Donna Wechsler Linden, *Off With their Perks*, FORBES, Dec. 4, 1995, at 54.

Donna Wechsler Linden & Robert Lenzner, *The Cosseted Director*, FORBES, May 22, 1995, at 168.

Jonathan R. Macey & Geoffrey P. Miller, Trans Union *Reconsidered*, 98 YALE L.J. 127 (1988).

Bayless Manning, *Reflections and Practical Tips on Life in the Boardroom After* Van Gorkom, 41 BUS. LAW. 1 (1985).

Bayless Manning, *The Business Judgment Rule and the Director's Duty of Attention: Time for Reality*, 39 BUS. LAW. 1477 (1984).

Nell Minow & Kit Bingham, *The Ideal Board*, THE CORP. BOARD, July 1993.

Robert Mundheim, *Some Thoughts on the Duties and Responsibilities of Unaffiliated Directors of Mutual Funds*, 155 U. PA. L. REV. 1058 (1967).

Philip Newman & Edward O'Dell, *Duties of Directors of Registered Investment Companies*, INVESTMENT COMPANY REGULATION AND COMPLIANCE, C131 ALI-ABA 83 (May 11, 1995).

William Nutt, *A Study of Mutual Fund Independent Directors*, 120 U. PA. L. REV. 179 (1971).

Alan R. Palmiter, *Mutual Fund Voting of Portfolio Shares: Why Not Disclose?*, 23 CARDOZO L. REV. 1419 (2002).

Michael Radmer, *Duties of the Directors of Investment Companies*, 3 J. CORP. L. 61 (1977).

Clarke Randall, *Fiduciary Duties of Investment Company Directors and Management Companies under the Investment Company Act of 1940*, 31 OKLA. L. REV. 635 (1978).

Richard Roberts, *Responsibilities of Investment Company Directors*, INV. LAW. 16 (1994).

Robert Robertson & Bradley Paulson, *Symposium: Regulation of Financial Derivatives: A Methodology for Mutual Fund Derivative Investments*, 1 STAN. J.L. BUS. & FIN. 237 (1995).

Peter Rodger, et al,. *Corporate Governance in the Global Mutual Fund Industry*, 28 INT'L BUS. LAW. 243 (2000).

William P. Rogers, Jr. & James N. Benedict, *Money Market Fund Management Fees: How Much Is Too Much*, 57 N.Y.U.L. REV. 1059 (1982).

Michael L. Sapir & James A. Bernstein, *Reorganization of Investment Companies*, 50 BUS. LAW. 817 (1995).

Victoria E. Schonfeld & Thomas M.J. Kerwin, *Organization of a Mutual Fund*, 49 BUS. LAW. 107 (1993).

Kenneth E. Scott, *What Role Is There for Independent Directors of Mutual Funds?*, 2 VILL. J.L. & INV. MGMT. 1 (2000), *available at* http://www.vls.villanova.edu/academics/vjlim/vol21.pdf.

James G. Smith, *Directors' Guide to Investment Company Adviser Fee Agreements and S36(B)*, 5 U. MIAMI BUS. L.J. 209 (1995).

Robert Stobaugh, *Director Compensation: A Lever to Improve Corporate Governance*, DIRECTOR'S MONTHLY, Aug. 1993, at 1.

James M. Storey & Thomas M. Clyde, *The Uneasy Chaperone. A Resource for Independent Directors of Mutual Funds*, MGMT. PRACTICE (2000).

David A. Sturms, *Enhancing the Effectiveness of Independent Directors: Is the System Broken, Creaking or Working?*, 1 VILL. J.L. & INV. MGMT. 103 (1999).

Mark Vander Broek, *The Demand Requirement in Investment Company Act Shareholder Actions*, 50 U. CHI. L. REV. 1500 (1983).

Earl D. Weiner & James J. Hanks, Jr., *Directors' Duties and the Discount*, 8 INV. LAW. 1 (2001).

Excessive Fee Cases

Since 1981, there have been six major Section 36(b) excessive advisory fee cases tried on the merits. In each case, the court held that there had not been a violation of Section 36(b). The court opinions in these cases, particularly the district court opinions, provide informative and interesting reading for independent directors and are well-illustrative of the nature of the deliberations that should be conducted by the directors. These cases are as follows:

Gartenberg v. Merrill Lynch Asset Mgmt., Inc., 528 F. Supp. 1038 (S.D.N.Y. 1981), *aff'd*, 694 F.2d 923 (2d Cir. 1982), *cert. denied*, 461 U.S. 906 (1983) (involving Merrill Lynch Ready Asset Trust).

Gartenberg v. Merrill Lynch Asset Mgmt., Inc., 573 F. Supp. 1293 (S.D.N.Y. 1982), *aff'd*, 740 F.2d 190 (2d Cir. 1984) (involving Merrill Lynch Ready Asset Trust).

Schuyt v. Rowe Price Prime Reserve Fund, Inc., 663 F. Supp. 962 (S.D.N.Y. 1987), *aff'd per curiam*, 835 F.2d 45 (2d Cir. 1987), *cert. denied*, 485 U.S. 1034 (1988).

Krinsk v. Fund Asset Mgmt., Inc., 715 F. Supp. 472 (S.D.N.Y. 1988), *aff'd*, 875 F.2d 404 (2d Cir.), *cert. denied*, 492 U.S. 919 (1989) (involving CMA Money Fund).

Kalish v. Franklin Advisers, Inc., 742 F. Supp. 1222 (S.D.N.Y. 1990), *aff'd*, 928 F.2d 590 (2d Cir.), *cert. denied*, 502 U.S. 818 (1991) (involving Franklin Custodian Funds, Inc.).

Krantz v. Fidelity Mgmt. & Research Co., 98 F. Supp. 2d 150 (D. Mass. 2000).